NOSH
FOR BUSY
MUMS & DADS

BY JOY MAY

@NOSHBOOKS

CONTENTS

LETTER FROM JOY

My sons have left home now, but visit frequently with their children, so I am now a busy Gran. I remember well the pressures of juggling work, bringing up children, looking after the home, etc. Add this to a tight budget and a busy husband, cooking was certainly a challenge. I would have loved to have had a book like this one, to inspire me and help me through those times.

My aim in this book is to help those of you who share similar stresses of feeding a family, even if your family setup is different to mine. Sometimes we can get into the rut of cooking the same things over and over, or reaching for the ready-made meals, or even pressing the button for a take-away! I want you to see how simple meals are possible and to inspire you to cook from fresh ingredients, with the result that your stress factors are minimised and you actually enjoy cooking for the family. I have included recipes that should take under 30 minutes to produce and some that may take 10 minutes to prepare and then sit in the oven for an hour or so. There are recipes that your kids can join in with and some especially designed for when the funds are low. All of these recipes should satisfy hungry tums.

For those of you with younger children, there are some tips on getting them to eat, not getting stressed when they don't, and some simple snacks for kids.

enjoy cooking

Joy

STORECUPBOARD

Here is a list of basics we suggest you keep in your storecupboard

FRIDGE

butter

spreads

milk

eggs

cheese, good, strong and tasty

mayo

stock, concentrated or cubes

lemons

FREEZER

spare loaf

packet of puff pastry

mince

chicken breast

peas

CUPBOARDS

olive oil

potatoes (stored in a bag)

onions (stored in a bag)

garlic (stored in a pot)

tinned chopped tomatoes

tinned tuna

baked beans

cannellini beans

sweetcorn

tomato purée

sun-dried tomatoes

couscous

spaghetti

pasta

rice, basmati

lentils

tomato sauce

flour, self-raising and plain

Worcestershire sauce

balsamic vinegar

white wine vinegar

soy sauce

assorted curry pastes

salt and pepper

pilau rice seasoning

mixed dried herbs

cinnamon

cumin

ground coriander

ground ginger

turmeric

paprika

chilli powder

honey

raisins

vanilla extract

sugar, granulated, brown and caster

fresh herbs, if you have a window sill!

GLUTEN-FREE

We recognise that there are more and more families dealing with allergies, such as gluten and wheat intolerances. For this reason, and the fact that we are fairly passionate about the whole subject of gluten, we have given some tips on how to adapt some of the recipes to avoid gluten and wheat products. In each recipe where you see the 'gluten-free option' icon, you will also see notes next to each ingredient which you need to make sure is gluten-free.

LABOUR SAVING EQUIPMENT

FOOD PROCESSOR

I would highly recommend getting a large, good quality processor. It will mix, slice, grate, liquidise, whip, not quite 'sing and dance', but will save a lot of time and energy.

HAND-HELD BLENDER

Great to get out quickly to liquidise soups, etc.

FOOD MIXER

Handy for egg whites, pancakes, small cakes, etc. Saves aching arms.

HOB-TO-OVEN CASSEROLE

Useful if you are cooking on the hob and later it goes in the oven. Saves washing-up a saucepan.

GOOD, THICK BOTTOMED SAUCEPANS

They are expensive, but will last for years and years. I have some and they are about 20 years old. They go in the dishwasher and come out as good as new.

2 NON-STICK FRYING PANS

If you are making cooked breakfast or pancakes, having two frying pans makes life so much easier.

LONG-HANDLED PLASTIC TONGS

Get the ones with the silicon ends and they will save scraping the non-stick off the pans. They are so easy to turn over things with.

GOOD SILICON SPATULAS AND COOKING SPOONS

Much more hygienic than wooden spoons and easy to clean.

A WOODEN AND A PLASTIC CHOPPING BOARD

Wood for normal stuff, plastic for fish or anything really smelly.

GOOD SHARP KNIVES.

Having a good sharp knife and a sharpener takes the labour out of chopping.

Collect them gradually, as they can be expensive. A chopping, paring knife and carving knife are all you really need.

AN EASY-PEELER

Don't keep using the one you have had for years. Buy a new, sharp one and take the toil out of any peeling you may feel necessary.

GOOD, STURDY, SHARP GRATER

If yours is dull and floppy, it will take forever to grate cheese and your arm is left aching and tired.

TEFLON SHEETS

Cost around £3 and last for ages. Really sticky stuff comes off in seconds and you are not left soaking and scrubbing baking or roasting trays.

NON-STICK WOK

The food cooks quicker than in a large saucepan, as there is more surface heat.

SAVING TIME

Time seems to be of the essence, so here are some things I have found really helpful.

EASY MEASURING

Learn how to measure using spoons and mugs, or your hand! The recipes in the book give tablespoon, dessertspoon, teaspoon and mug measures. The mug is ½ pint. I keep a mug handy all the time I cook, much easier and quicker than using scales. The illustration on the next page shows the size of the mug.

PREPARE WELL BEFORE YOU START

Gather together all your ingredients before you start cooking. This way, you won't be running around looking for things as you cook. Clear your work surfaces of as much 'stuff' as possible and just have the really important things out.

HALVE YOUR TIME AND EFFORT

Cook double and freeze. If you know you want to use a meal from the freezer in the evening, get it out in the morning and leave in the fridge throughout the day. This way, it should be almost defrosted by the time you come to use it. Throughout the book I have noted the recipes which are good for freezing. Tips on freezing can be found on our website: noshbooks.com/freezing.

LET THE SUPERMARKET DO THE WORK

Buy groceries online. If I have a list, I can shop online in 10 minutes, whilst it takes an hour to go to the supermarket. You may want to go to the shops for an outing, but it takes time and energy. Delivery charges can be very small and it may cost you less than the petrol to get to the supermarket. Use our new NOSH App to create your weekly menus and shopping lists (see p14) — it will save so much time.

DON'T WASTE TIME WAITING FOR WATER TO BOIL

Boil water for veggies, pasta or rice in the kettle, not the pan. Put the kettle on before you start cooking.

SHORT PREP, LONG COOK

Slow-cook recipes often require little preparation, just a long time in the oven, e.g. 'Sweet Pork & Apple Stew' (see p102) and 'Beef & Mushroom Casserole' (see p124).

ENLIST HELP

Use spouses or kids, if they are available. Be specific about what they can do, e.g. chop things, wash things up, set the table, etc. Get a step-up, or stool, so younger kids can be involved. Short term, kids may seem to get in the way, but, long term, they need to be able to cook and will be a help.

IN THE PEACE AND QUIET

If you have a small baby, cook when they are 'napping'. Much less frustrating than when they are awake and require your attention.
Buy things like pastry. When the children are older you will have a lifetime to make pastry, bread and all those 'homely' things.

What is quicker than just grabbing a mug and filling it? What is easier to remember as a unit of measure than a mug of this, or 2 mugs of that?

This book is designed so that you don't need to use weighing scales, but we have included the gram/millilitre measures for those of you who prefer a bit more precision.

Throughout the book I have used a mug to measure ingredients. This mug holds ½ pint or 300ml of liquid and is the exact size of the mug pictured opposite. So find a mug that measures up to this one and you won't go far wrong.

This actual mug is the same one I used when writing my first book back in 2000. It has a place in my heart. Although it is now cracked, it still has a special spot in our mug cupboard!

OUR MUG

ACTUAL SIZE

SAVING MONEY

SHOP AT COSTCO ETC.

Try shopping at wholesale supermarkets. If you don't qualify, you can get a card on a friend's account. You need to buy in bulk, but many things are significantly cheaper.

MAKE YOUR OWN PACKED LUNCHES

Make for yourselves and for the children. To make a wholemeal bread, ham, lettuce and mayo sandwich costs approximately £1 in total. To buy a ready-made ham salad sandwich is around £2.20. This is a saving of £6 per week, per person. See 'packed lunches section' (see p34).

USE THINGS UP AT THE END OF THE WEEK

At the end of the week, use the veg that's coming towards the end of its life in dishes like 'Roasted Sweet Potato Soup' (see p44), or 'Chicken and Roast Vegetable Couscous' (see p66).

FREEZE LEFTOVERS

If you just have enough left for one portion, freeze it. Save up the single portions till you have enough for everyone to have their choice and you have a 'no-cook' night.

BREAD

Put whole, sliced loaves in the freezer and only get bread out when you need it, as it is so quick to defrost. This way you don't waste the dried-up slices and you always have fresh bread.

MAKE SOUPS

This is inexpensive and often packed with great vegetables.

'COST UP' YOUR WEEKLY SHOP

If you are on a tight budget, it is helpful to plan your menu. To help you do this, we have a FREE menu and shopping list app. In the app, and in this book, we price up every meal, so hopefully you won't have any surprises when you get to the till. The prices in this book are correct as of **October 2020** (ave. of Tesco and Sainsbury's).

BUY SPICES IN BULK

Buy the refill bags and store in airtight jars. They will keep for ages. The Natco brand is available at Sainsbury's, most Asian supermarkets and online at www. natco-online.com

YOUR FREE NOSH BOOKS APP

To help you plan and shop for your food, we have designed a free app to create menus and shopping lists. Simply browse any of our books and add recipes of your choice to a weekly menu. Then the app does all the tedious work of creating the shopping list for you and boom! You are ready to shop.

No more aimless wandering around the supermarket, only to get home and still not be able to make a meal. What have you got to lose, download it for FREE.

SCAN ME

SLOW-COOK R...

NOTE: When choosing p...
The fat contains lots of...
liquid before making th...

ONE MORE THING: If you wa...
greased baking tray. Pu...

1kg piece of **pork shoulder**

1 eating **apple**, cored and cut into 8

1 **onion**, cut into 8

1 teaspoon **fennel seeds**

2 mugs **water**

4 large **potatoes**, peeled and cut into 4cm chunks

6 **carrots**, peeled and cut into 4cm pieces

2 tablespoons **oil**

1 head of **broccoli**

25g softened **butter** (measure using packet)

1 tablespoon **flour**

120

ONE-POT BEEF COBBLER

£1.04 PER PERSON | SERVES 4 | EASE ★★★★☆ | PREP 20 mins | COOK 50 mins

NOTE: This is a really homely dish. Great for winter evenings to warm your cockles!

WHERE ON EARTH: Suet can be found with the flour in the 'baking section' of the supermarket.

1 tablespoon **oil**

2 **onions**, sliced

500g **beef mince**

4 medium **carrots**, chopped small

1 tablespoon **flour**

1 mug defrosted **frozen peas**

6 **mushrooms**, sliced

2 mugs **water** + 1 **beef stock pot/cube**

1 teaspoon dried **mixed herbs**

salt and **pepper**

DUMPLING TOPPING

1½ mugs **self-raising flour**

¾ mug **suet**

pinch **salt**

1 teaspoon freeze dried **basil** or **coriander**

¾ mug **water**

1 beaten **egg**

1 Preheat the oven to 180°C fan oven/200°C/gas 6.

2 Heat the oil in a hob-to-oven casserole. Fry the onion in the oil until soft.

3 Add the mince and carrots and cook until the meat is no longer pink. Add the flour and stir well.

4 Add the peas, mushrooms, water, stock, herbs, salt and pepper. Stir well and simmer for 10 minutes.

5 To make the dumpling top, put the flour, suet, salt and herbs in a dish and stir well. Add water a little at a time and mix. Add just enough water to make a soft ball.

6 Put some flour onto a board or plate. Turn out the mixture and form a ball.

7 Cut into eight pieces and form each into a ball.

8 Gently place them on the top of the meat mixture and brush the top with beaten egg, or milk, to help it brown.

9 Bake in the oven for 25–30 minutes, or until the crust is browned.

JOE & SARAH: "This was my first time making dumplings. They were suprisingly easy and so very tasty that you would have thought I had spent a lot of time making this dish."

122

MENU 1

MONDAY
BACON AND MOZZARELLA
PASTA BAKE - P69

TUESDAY
BEEF AND POTATO HOT POT
- P72

WEDNESDAY
SUPER SIMPLE TUNA BAKE
- P171

THURSDAY
ONE-POT CHICKEN HOT POT
- P188

FRIDAY
PASTITSIO - P204

SATURDAY
EGG-FRIED PLOUGHMAN'S
- P94 (LUNCH)
SPICED CHICKEN AND HERB
COUSCOUS - P154 (DINNER)

SUNDAY
SLOW-COOK ROAST PORK
- P120

SHOPPING LIST

- ☐ 13 Medium potatoes
- ☐ 2 sweet potatoes
- ☐ 15 tomatoes
- ☐ 4 onions
- ☐ 1 yellow pepper
- ☐ 1 red onion
- ☐ green veg for 1 meal
- ☐ 1 apple
- ☐ 10 carrots
- ☐ 1 head broccoli
- ☐ bunch spring onions
- ☐ 2 lemons
- ☐ garlic
- ☐ fresh basil
- ☐ fresh coriander
- ☐ 300g smoked streaky bacon
- ☐ 750g minced beef
- ☐ 500g minced beef
- ☐ 8 boneless chicken thighs
- ☐ 3 chicken breasts
- ☐ 1kg piece pork shoulder
- ☐ 1kg Cheddar cheese
- ☐ 300ml double cream
- ☐ 300ml soured cream
- ☐ 200g feta cheese
- ☐ 2 balls mozzarella
- ☐ 4 eggs
- ☐ frozen peas

- ☐ sun-dried tomatoes
- ☐ 2 small packets crisps
- ☐ tin baked beans
- ☐ tin chopped tomatoes
- ☐ 2 tins tuna
- ☐ 1 wholemeal loaf
- ☐ 1 pint milk

Check cupboards
- ☐ pasta (3 meals)
- ☐ oil
- ☐ stock cubes
- ☐ tomato purée
- ☐ Worcestershire sauce
- ☐ salt and pepper
- ☐ butter
- ☐ dried basil
- ☐ flour
- ☐ mixed herbs
- ☐ HP sauce
- ☐ pickle
- ☐ cumin
- ☐ ground coriander
- ☐ paprika
- ☐ couscous
- ☐ fennel seeds

**TRY OUR FREE APP
TO HELP PLAN
YOUR OWN MENU**

SCAN ME

MENU 2

MONDAY
HONEY CHICKEN BAKE - P64

TUESDAY
GINGER CHICKEN STIR - FRY - P76

WEDNESDAY
BALSAMIC CHILLI BEEF RAGU - P84

THURSDAY
BANGERS AND SWEET POTATO MASH - P136

FRIDAY
CHORIZO AND PANCETTA BAKE - P70

SATURDAY
GRILLED TUNA BAGELS - P40 (LUNCH)

MOROCCAN LAMB PIE - P100 (DINNER)

SUNDAY
CREAMY PORK AND MUSHROOM STEW - P112

SHOPPING LIST

- [ ] Savoy cabbage
- [ ] 10 potatoes
- [ ] celery
- [ ] 10 carrots
- [ ] piece of fresh ginger (for 2 meals)
- [ ] 7 onions
- [ ] 2 courgettes
- [ ] 19 mushrooms
- [ ] 4 tomatoes
- [ ] 1 lemon
- [ ] 2 bunches spring onions
- [ ] 2 sweet potatoes
- [ ] 2 fat red chillies
- [ ] 1 red pepper
- [ ] 2 yellow pepper
- [ ] 1 broccoli
- [ ] fresh coriander
- [ ] fresh basil
- [ ] fresh parsley
- [ ] 6 chicken breasts
- [ ] 750g stewing pork
- [ ] 500g lamb mince
- [ ] 500g minced beef
- [ ] 100g pack pancetta lardons
- [ ] 8 large sausages
- [ ] pkt streaky bacon
- [ ] 4 small chorizo sausages
- [ ] 400g pack fresh or straight-to-wok egg noodles
- [ ] 750g Cheddar cheese
- [ ] 300ml double cream
- [ ] small piece of Parmesan
- [ ] 8 eggs
- [ ] 4 bagels
- [ ] 2 tins tuna
- [ ] 3 tins tomatoes
- [ ] baked beans
- [ ] small wholemeal loaf

Check cupboards
- [ ] flour
- [ ] paprika
- [ ] mixed herbs
- [ ] dried thyme
- [ ] ground coriander
- [ ] cumin
- [ ] golden syrup
- [ ] oil
- [ ] butter
- [ ] stock cubes
- [ ] tomato purée
- [ ] bread
- [ ] cornflour
- [ ] sugar
- [ ] mayo
- [ ] honey
- [ ] soy
- [ ] garlic (6 cloves)
- [ ] olives
- [ ] white wine vinegar
- [ ] toasted sesame oil
- [ ] balsamic vinegar
- [ ] Worcestershire Sauce
- [ ] penne pasta

HOW MUCH SHOULD MY CHILD BE EATING?

Try not to concentrate too much on just the quantity of food your child is consuming. Appetites will vary from child to child and forcing them to eat the (sometimes) arbitrary amount of food that we put on their plate can be an unhelpful starting point. One very rough guide (if you are looking for one), is simply the size of a child's plate — no need to pile it full to overflowing! Also, we don't need to obsess over 'finishing a plate of food' every mealtime. Instead, focus on what they are eating and the kind of relationship they are developing with food.

WHAT IF THEY WON'T EAT?

Having a 'fussy eater' is really hard, if that is your current experience, but you are not alone. Lots of children will have phases of being picky. Just try to remember that it is just that, a phase. One of the simplest places to start, is making sure they haven't filled up between meals on snacks or sweet drinks. Try limiting how much of these types of food you keep in the house if they/you find it too tempting.

START YOUNG.

Exposing children to a variety of flavours as early as possible is great. When weaning, try blitzed-up portions of your meals if they are nice and varied. Remember to take out their portion before you add the salt.

MAKE FOOD ATTRACTIVE.

If everything looks bland, it is unlikely to be appealing to kids. Bright coloured vegetables help to brighten up plates of food. You might need to experiment with chopping things up small, if you think certain textures of vegetable (like mushrooms and onions) are off-putting.

MAKE FOOD TASTY.

This may seem obvious, but make sure you are not expecting your children to eat something that you wouldn't want to eat yourself. One way to make veggies tasty, for example, is to roast them rather than just boiling them.

ENCOURAGE TRYING NEW THINGS.

Keep introducing different foods and don't give up the first time they refuse. Don't overwhelm them with new things though. Encourage them to try at least a mouthful of something they have not tried before.

Praise this kind of thing over 'finishing off their plate'.

GETTING KIDS INVOLVED.

Cooking (and even shopping) with kids can help massively. There are a few recipes in the book where I suggest that children can help, even from the toddler age. It may seem time-consuming in the food prep stage, but it can pay off if your child feels involved in the process from start to finish.

MAKE MEAL-TIMES SPECIAL.

Make it part of your routine to eat together as much as possible. Children learn a huge amount from seeing us as parents eat well and it creates a more relaxed atmosphere if you are all around the table chatting and being 'normal'.

DON'T MAKE FOOD A BATTLEGROUND.

Don't pile on the pressure. Remain as calm as possible, saying things like "this is what we are eating. It is OK if you don't want it,

but there will be nothing else until the next meal". Let them leave the table, but don't give them anything else, however much they protest.

PRAISE AND ENCOURAGEMENT.

It can be tough at times to to encourage your child when they have eaten hardly anything and 'simply' tried one solitary mouthful of something new, but stick at it. Look for the glimmers of hope and praise those. You might also want to think about what 'currency' works best with your child in encouraging them to eat. One thing to be wary of using, in this instance, is a reward like junk food. We have all been there: "eat this last mouthful of broccoli and I'll give you this packet of sweets". Remember what you are aiming for — healthy children with good relationships with food.

PERFECT RICE EVERY TIME

I would recommend that you use basmati rice, as it consistently cooks well.

RICE FOR 1 ADULT = ½ MUG RICE + 1 MUG WATER

(+ 1 teaspoon of pilau rice seasoning. Optional, but gives a yummy flavour)

1 Boil the water in a kettle, add the measured amount of water to the pan. Add the seasoning and stir.

2 Add the rice and stir once. Bring back to the boil and simmer gently. Put the lid on the pan and cook for approximately 10 minutes. Do not stir while the rice is cooking, or you will make it sticky.

3 Test the rice once the water has boiled away. If the rice is still too crunchy, and the water has all gone, then you have boiled it too quickly. Add a little more water, replace the lid and cook for another 5 minutes.

HOW TO COOK PASTA

There are innumerable kinds of pasta to choose from in the shops, made from different ingredients. Most will have instructions on the packets as to how to cook them. Just in case you have lost the packet, here are some general guidelines:

spaghetti measure

4
3
2
1

SPAGHETTI

1 Half-fill a large saucepan with boiling water.

2 Lower the spaghetti sticks into the water. Once the half that is in the water has softened slightly, push the other half in. Simmer for 6–8 minutes.

3 Drain the water off and add one teaspoon of butter, or olive oil, to stop the spaghetti sticking together.

MOST OTHER PASTAS

Again, boil enough water to cover the pasta. Once the water is boiling, add the pasta. One mug of dried pasta is plenty for one person with a very healthy appetite. Simmer for the appropriate time, drain and add butter, or olive oil, to prevent the pasta sticking together.
As a rough guide, here are some timings for various pastas:

Tagliatelle (4–5 mins)
Radiatore (10 mins)
Fusilli (6–8 mins)
Penne (10–12 mins)

Conchiglie (7–8 mins)
Macaroni (12–15 mins)
Farfalle (6–8 mins)

ALL THINGS POTATOES

ROAST POTATOES

Serves 4 if you use 6 medium potatoes

1 Preheat the oven to 180°C fan/200°C/gas 6. Cut the potatoes into 5cm chunks. You do not need to peel the potatoes.

2 Place them on a baking tray. Sprinkle with salt, pepper and olive oil. If you have some fresh rosemary, pull off the leaves and sprinkle over the potatoes (dried rosemary will also work fine).

3 Using your hands, make sure the oil is evenly distributed around the potatoes. Make sure that the potatoes are not flat-side down, as this will mean more of the potatoes will brown.

4 Cook in the oven for 55 minutes until they are brown.

MINI ROAST POTATOES

This a great way to make roast potatoes in a short time. They will cook in the time it takes to make the rest of a meal. Serves 4 if you use 6 medium potatoes.

1 Preheat the oven to 200°C fan/ 220°C/gas 7.

2 Cut the potatoes into 2cm cubes. You don't need to peel them.

3 Place them on a baking tray, drizzle with olive oil and season with salt and pepper. Mix together with your hands and spread out.

4 Place in the oven for 30 minutes until browned.

5 You can sprinkle some dried rosemary over the potatoes if you wish.

AMAZING WEDGES

1 Preheat the oven to 180°C fan/200°C/gas 6 . Cut the potatoes into wedges.

2 Place on baking trays and sprinkle with olive oil and salt and pepper. Distribute the oil well with your hands.

3 Make sure that each wedge is 'standing up', not sitting on a flat side. You will get nice brown wedges this way and they won't stick to the tray as much.

4 Place in the oven for 25–30 minutes, or until browned.

POSH ROAST POTATOES

Serves 4 if you use 6 medium potatoes

1 Preheat the oven to 180°C fan/200°C/gas 6. Peel the potatoes and cut into 5cm chunks.

2 Place in a pan of boiling, salted water and cook for 10 minutes.

3 Place a baking tray in the oven with 2 tablespoons of vegetable oil on it.

4 Drain the potatoes and return to the pan. Put the lid on the pan and shake it quite vigorously. This will cause the outsides of the potatoes to become a little furry.

5 Place the potatoes on the heated baking tray and carefully turn them to distribute the oil.

6 Put in the oven for 45–50 minutes, until browned.

BASIC MASH

6 **medium potatoes**, peeled

25g cube **butter** (measure using packet)

1 Cut the potatoes into 5cm chunks.

2 Put the potatoes into boiling, salted water. Once the water has come back to the boil, turn down the heat, put a lid on the pan and cook for approximately 10 minutes.

3 Test after 10 minutes. If cooked, drain the water off. If not cooked, boil for a little longer, taking care not to overcook, or the potatoes will disintegrate in the water.

4 Add the butter and mash with a potato masher.

5 Mash until all the lumps have gone, but don't work the mash too much as it will become glutinous. Add salt and freshly ground pepper.

MORE THAN MASH

'Mash' has had old-fashioned connotations for many years, but is making a definite comeback in modern cooking, rarely as 'simple mash'. Here are some ways to spice it up:

CHEDDAR AND MUSTARD MASH

At the 'mashing stage', add ½ mug grated, mature Cheddar cheese, together with 1 good teaspoon of wholegrain mustard, salt and freshly ground black pepper. The wholegrain mustard also gives an attractive look to the mash.

SWEET POTATO MASH

Just use half normal potatoes and half sweet potatoes.

POTATO CRUSH

6–8 **medium potatoes**

1 Put boiled water in a large saucepan. Bring back to the boil.

2 Cut unpeeled, washed potatoes into 2cm chunks. Add to the boiling water, season with salt and bring back to the boil. Cover with a lid and simmer for 10 minutes.

3 Drain and return the to the pan.

4 Add a good chunk of butter. You can add a mug of grated cheese at this point. Use a potato masher and just squash the potatoes. Don't completely mash them, keep them 'rustic'. Stir with a spoon to distribute the butter and the cheese if you have used it. Put the lid back on the pan to keep warm until needed.

JACKET POTATOES

Jacket potatoes make a very easy meal. You can make them much more interesting than by just adding beans or cheese. Use medium or large potatoes. Always make a cut in the skin with a knife before baking, or it may explode in the oven or the microwave. You will only get the crisp jackets if you cook the potato in the oven. Timing depends on the size of the potato.

Oven baked — Preheat the oven to 200°C fan/220°C/gas 7 and bake for 50–60 minutes.

Microwave and oven — Preheat the oven to 200°C fan/220°C/gas 7. Cook in the microwave on full power for 5 minutes and then in the oven for 30 minutes.

Microwave — 7–10 minutes on full power.

BACON AND BEANS

Fry 6 **smoked bacon rashers** until they are crisp. Remove from the pan and chop into small strips (scissors work well for this). Chop an **onion** and fry until it begins to brown. Add to one **tin of beans**, together with 1 teaspoon **brown sugar** and 1 tablespoon **Worcestershire sauce**. Serves 4.

SWEET POTATO BAKES

Bake in the same way as normal potatoes. Mix together 1/2 x 200g pack of **feta cheese** with 3 chopped **spring onions**, 1/2 a **fat red chilli**, deseeded and chopped, zest of a **lemon** and 2 **tomatoes**, chopped. Season well and share amongst the potatoes. Serves 2–3.

TUNA, SWEETCORN AND MAYO

Mix together a **tin of tuna** with 1 tablespoon of **mayo** and a 340g tin of **sweetcorn**. Season well. Serves 4. Any leftovers can be used in sandwiches.

COOKED CHICKEN AND MAYONNAISE

Pan roast a couple of **chicken breasts**, see p66. One minute before the end of the cooking time, spread a dessertspoon of **curry paste** over the chicken. Slice the chicken and mix with 1 tablespoon of **mayo** and 2 chopped **spring onions**. Serves 4.

SALAMI AND RED PEPPER

Chop 3 slices of not-too-spicy **salami** plus 1 **ready-roasted, red pepper** (from a jar) and 2 tablespoons **crème fraîche**. Serves 2–3.

SALMON AND SOURED CREAM

Mix a 120g packet of **smoked salmon trimmings** with a 300g pot of **soured cream** and 1 tablespoon of **freshly chopped mixed herbs** (basil works fine on its own). Season with **salt** and **pepper** and share between the potatoes. Serves 4.

STUFF ON TOAST

CHEESE ON TOAST

Use different kinds of cheese: Cheddar, Gruyère Brie, Mozzarella, etc. Add things to go under the cheese, such as ham, pickle, Marmite, or sliced tomatoes. Slice or grate the cheese and place on top. Make sure the cheese covers the edges of the toast; it will protect the corners of the bread from being burned.

TUNA

Mix a can of tuna with 1 tablespoon mayo and season well with salt and pepper. Spread over the toasted bread and put grated Cheddar over the top. Grill until the cheese begins to brown.

SALMON

Mix a tin of salmon with 3 chopped spring onions. Spread over the toast. Mix 1 small pot of cottage cheese with 1 mug of grated Cheddar cheese and spread over the salmon. Grill until the cheese begins to brown.

BEANS ON TOAST WITH EGG ON TOP

Toast the bread, heat the beans, and then fry or poach the eggs (p92). Great with HP sauce.

INTERESTING SANDWICHES

One way to make sandwiches more interesting is to vary the bread you use. Try to avoid white bread all the time, as all the good stuff has been taken out and some not so good stuff added in! Choose different kinds of wholemeal or granary loaves, bread buns or pitta breads.

BEEF WITH CREAM CHEESE AND SUN-DRIED TOMATO

Mix a finely chopped, sun-dried tomato with about 150g cream cheese. Spread on one slice of bread and add the sliced beef and some lettuce.

COTTAGE CHEESE & BANANA

Spread the bread with a liberal amount of honey or jam and top with cottage cheese. Slice a banana and pile into the sandwich. Squash the other slice of bread on top to keep everything together.

TUNA & HARD-BOILED EGG

Drain a 160g tin of tuna. Put half in a bowl. Hard-boil 2 eggs (see video link below). Peel and chop and add to the bowl. Chop 2 spring onions and add to the bowl with 1 tablespoon of mayo. Mix together and season well.

EGG MAYO

Hard-boil 2 eggs (see video link below). Rinse them under cold water, remove the shells and chop them up. Mix together with 1 tablespoon of mayo and season with salt and pepper.

BACON & BANANA

Grill or fry 3 slices of streaky bacon until crisp. Put in the sandwich with a sliced banana.

CHICKEN, MAYO & LETTUCE

If you have roasted a chicken and have some spare, cut it into small pieces. Spread mayo over one slice of bread and add the lettuce. Season with salt and pepper. Add the chicken on top and place the other slice of bread on top.

BACON & BRIE

Grill or fry 3 slices of streaky bacon until crisp. Slice the Brie, add to the sandwich and serve whilst the bacon is still hot.

SMOKED SALMON & CREAM CHEESE

Use the thin sandwich slices of smoked salmon. Spread one slice with cream cheese, add some sliced cucumber and a sliced spring onion, along with the smoked salmon.

SCRAMBLED EGGS & CHEESE AND TOMATO

Grate 1/2 mug of cheese. Chop a tomato, quite finely. Heat a little butter in a small non-stick saucepan, add the tomatoes and fry for 1 minute. Add 2 beaten eggs and cook until they begin to set, stirring steadily. Take off the heat, add the cheese and stir. Season well and make the sandwich whilst the eggs are still hot.

WATCH OUR 'BOIL AN EGG' VIDEO
NOSHBOOKS.COM/BOIL-AN-EGG

SALADS

These salads can be served with many of the recipes as an alternative to the ones suggested. They are also great to use with barbecues. Once you get into making salads, you can vary these to your taste and even begin to make up your own.

£0.20 /PERSON

£0.29 /PERSON

£0.49 /PERSON

MINTY POTATO SALAD

4 medium **potatoes**, cut into small chunks, or 8 new potatoes

2 tablespoons **crème fraîche** or **soured cream**

3 tablespoons **Greek yogurt**

4 **spring onions**, chopped

2 tablespoons freshly chopped **mint** or 1 teaspoon **dried mint**

salt and **pepper**

Cook the potatoes for 10 minutes. Leave to cool and then mix all the ingredients together.

CARROT AND APPLE SALAD

1 large **carrot**

2 **red eating apples**

2 **spring onions**

1 tablespoon freshly chopped **basil**

2 tablespoons **olive oil**

juice of a **lemon**

salt and **pepper**

Put the carrots, apples, onions and basil through the coarse grater of the food processor. Alternatively, grate the carrot and apple and chop the onions and basil. Mix together with the oil and lemon juice and season well.

RICE SALAD

3/4 mug (190g) **basmati rice** + 1 teaspoon **pilau seasoning** (optional)

1 mug defrosted **frozen peas**

1 **apple**, unpeeled, cored and chopped into chunks

2 sticks **celery**, chopped

2 tablespoons **raisins**

1 tablespoon freshly chopped **basil**

3 **spring onions**, chopped

3 tablespoons **mayo**

1 tablespoon **olive oil**

juice of a **lemon**

Cook the rice and add the peas to the pan 2 minutes before the end of the cooking time. Leave to cool. Mix the rest of the ingredients together.

£0.32 /PERSON

£0.46 /PERSON

£0.61 /PERSON

GREEN SALAD WITH CROUTONS

1 tablespoon **olive oil**

2 slices **wholemeal bread**

1 **Little Gem lettuce**, sliced

2 **spring onions**, sliced

1 tablespoon freshly chopped **basil**

2 sticks **celery**, finely sliced

1 **green apple**, finely sliced

grated **Parmesan**

Heat the oil in a frying pan and add the bread. Fry on both sides until browned. Cut into small squares. Mix with the rest of the ingredients and sprinkle the Parmesan over the top.

COUSCOUS SALAD

1/2 mug **couscous**

4 **spring onions**, chopped

1 tablespoon freshly chopped **parsley**

1 tablespoon freshly chopped **basil**

340g tin **sweetcorn**

1 **red pepper**, finely chopped

2 tablespoons **olive oil**

juice and zest of a **lemon**

1 teaspoon **granulated sugar**

salt and **pepper**

Put the couscous in a bowl and add 1 mug of boiling, salted water. Put a plate over and leave to stand for 4 minutes. Leave to cool slightly and add the rest of the ingredients. Mix together.

CELERY, FENNEL AND APPLE SALAD

2 **Little Gem lettuces**, finely sliced

4 **spring onions**, chopped

1/2 **fennel bulb**, finely sliced

1 **red apple**, cored and finely sliced

2 sticks **celery**, finely sliced

8cm piece **cucumber**, cut into thin strips

DRESSING

salt and **pepper**

2 tablespoons **extra virgin olive oil**

juice of a **lemon**

1 teaspoon **granulated sugar**

Mix the salad ingredients together. Mix the dressing together, pour over and distribute well.

LUNCH BOXES

Lunch boxes don't need to be a chore, or have the same old things in every day. You will be bored and the kids will also be bored. Ask your children what others have in their lunch boxes and you may find some ideas you want to copy. Most lunch boxes will contain a sandwich, fruit, drink and a chocolate/fruity bar, but there are variations to be made on this theme.

SANDWICHES

If you find that you get the crusts back every day, then just cut them off in the first place. If you have the patience, cut the sandwiches into shapes. The fillings can be quite simple: ham, chicken, tuna, etc. Salad will have gone soggy by lunchtime and, if you give them eggs, other kids will complain about the smell! Put a few carrot or cucumber sticks, tiny cheese cubes or cherry tomatoes with the sandwiches.

FRUIT IS GREAT

Apples, bananas, grapes and peeled satsumas work well. Some children like dried fruit, such as raisins or apricots. An alternative to this is to put some fruit in jelly and give them a portion each day — either fresh strawberries etc, or use packets of preserved fruit, or tinned fruit. Tinned fruit is better than no fruit. Choose the jelly without sugar added. The jelly and fruit will last about 3 days.

YOGURT

You can buy the small pots, but a cheaper way is to have a small clip-top box (easy for them to open) with natural yogurt and a few pieces of frozen fruit, plus some honey in it (see photo opposite). Come lunch-time the fruit will be defrosted and they can give it a stir.

FRUIT BARS/CAKES

You can freeze 'Fruit Muffins' (see p226), or 'Apricot Flap Jacks' (see p223) and just bring out enough for each day. They will be thawed by lunchtime, but also serve to keep the rest of the lunchbox cool.

DRINKS

Boxed drinks are the easiest, or you can buy an easily-sealed drink bottle and fill it each day.
Another idea is to make Friday a treat day, so the lunch box may include a chocolate bar, or a bag of crisps.

PASTRY

If you have never made pastry before, here is an easy recipe for shortcrust pastry. I never seem to have the time to make puff pastry and always buy that ready-made. Shortcrust, however, is simple when you know how and here is the 'know how'!

175g **butter**, cold from the fridge (measure using packet)

1 ³/₄ mugs (340g) **plain flour**

1 beaten **egg**

¹/₄ mug (75ml) **water**

1   Cut the butter into small pieces and add the flour.

2   Rub in the butter and flour using your fingers and thumbs. Don't use the palms of your hands, as they will be warm. Keep going until the mixture resembles breadcrumbs. Alternatively, place in a food-processor or food-mixer, on slow speed and let it do the work for you. Either way, don't over mix.

3   Add sufficient egg and water to make a soft dough. Turn out onto a floured board and squash together. Handle as little as possible; don't knead the dough, save that for bread.

4   Pop in the fridge for 30 minutes.

5   Put back onto the floured board and roll out with even movements. Keep turning the dough, so that the edges stay the same thickness as the middle.

6   Pull the pastry back over the rolling-pin and place on the casserole or flan dish.

Pastry is usually baked at 180°C fan/200°C/gas 6, but this may change according to the contents of the dish.

QUICK BITES

Saturday lunch-time, kids home from school, or on school holidays, not much time, but everyone hungry? Here are a few inexpensive and quick ideas to feed the hungry hordes. Some of these recipes you can freeze beforehand, to be prepared for those busy days.

GRILLED TUNA BAGELS

4 **bagels**, sliced

2 x 160g tin **tuna**, drained

2 tablespoons **mayo**

juice of ½ **lemon**

8 **spring onions**, chopped

2 mugs (150g) grated **Cheddar cheese**

1 Lightly toast the bagels.

2 Mix the tuna, mayo, lemon juice and onions together. Place on the bottom half of the bagels and sprinkle with the grated cheese.

3 Place under a hot grill until the cheese melts.

£2.55 /TOTAL

SERVES 4

EASE ★★☆☆☆

PREP 15 MINS

COOK 15 MINS

HAM AND CHEESE PINWHEELS

375g packet **ready-rolled puff pastry**

3 slices thick **ham**, or quite a few slices of the wafer-thin stuff.

1 mug (75g) grated **Cheddar cheese**

2 **spring onions**, chopped

1 beaten **egg**

1   Preheat the oven to 200°C fan/220°C/gas 7. Grease a large baking tray.

2   Unroll the pastry sheet and place the sliced ham over the pastry. Sprinkle the cheese and onion evenly over the ham. Season with salt and pepper (You can make this recipe using chopped, uncooked bacon and half a chopped onion, instead of the ham and spring onions. This will give a stronger taste).

3   Roll up lengthways into a 'long sausage' and cut into 1cm slices. Lay them flat on the baking tray.

4   Brush the tops with the beaten egg and place in the oven for 15 minutes, or until browned.

SWEET POTATO AND LENTIL SOUP

2 tablespoons **olive oil**

2 **red onions**, sliced

3 cloves **garlic**, chopped

4 medium **sweet potatoes**, peeled and cut into chunks

1 dessertspoon **mild curry paste** (GF option)

4 mugs (1200ml) **water**

½ mug (125g) **red lentils**

1 **vegetable stock cube/pot** (GF option)

1 **apple**, cored, peeled and chopped roughly

juice of a **lemon**

1 tablespoon freshly chopped **coriander**

1 Heat the oil in a large saucepan and add the onions, garlic and sweet potatoes. Fry until they begin to soften.

2 Add the curry paste, water, lentils, stock and apple. Bring to the boil, then turn down to simmer for 20 minutes.

3 Blend with a hand-held blender until smooth. Add the lemon juice and coriander. Season. If the soup is really thick, add a little more water.

HONEY, CARROT AND LEEK SOUP

75g **butter** (measure using packet)

3 **leeks**, sliced

8 large **carrots**, roughly chopped

1 tablespoon **honey**

½ teaspoon **paprika**

2 **bay leaves**

4 mugs (1200ml) **water**

2 **vegetable stock cubes/pots** (GF option)

bread (GF option)

Cheddar cheese

sweet pickle

1. Melt the butter in a large saucepan over a medium heat. Add the leeks to the pan and fry for 2–3 minutes until they begin to soften.

2. Add the carrots, honey, paprika and bay leaves. Cook for 2 minutes.

3. Pour in the water and the stock. Bring to the boil and then simmer for 25 minutes. Take out the bay leaves, blend the soup and season to taste.

4. Serve with cheese on toast, with the pickle spread under the cheese, cut into 'soldiers'.

 £0.45 /PERSON   SERVES 4   EASE ★★★☆☆   PREP 10 MINS   COOK 30 MINS   V GF OPTION

ROASTED SWEET POTATO SOUP

This is ideal for using up the leftover veggies that lurk in the fridge at the end of the week. Cooking double and freezing for another day makes sense too.

ONE MORE THING: To blend your soup, it is best if you have a hand-held blender, or you could use a food processor.

1 large **sweet potato**, peeled and cut into chunks

2 **carrots**, peeled and cut into strips

6 **tomatoes**, cut in half

1 **onion**, cut into wedges

2 tablespoons **olive oil**

1 sprig **fresh rosemary** leaves, or 1 teaspoon **dried rosemary**

4 mugs (1200ml) **boiling water**

1 **vegetable stock cube** (GF option)

serve with **croutons**, see p33 (GF option)

1 Preheat the oven to 200°C fan/220°C/gas 7.

2 Put the vegetables on a large roasting tin or baking tray. Sprinkle with the oil and rosemary. Season well and mix everything up with your hands, leaving the tomatoes face up. Spread everything evenly on the tray. Put in the oven for 30 minutes.

3 Once the vegetables are nicely browned, tip them and their juices into a saucepan, with 3½ mugs of water and the stock. Blitz, but not too much.

4 Bring to the boil. Add the other ½ mug of water, if necessary. The soup should be quite thick and not watery. Take off the heat and taste for seasoning.

5 Serve with some crusty bread, or croutons, see p33.

£0.92 /PERSON · SERVES 4 · EASE ★★☆☆☆ · PREP 20 MINS · COOK 10 MINS · OK TO FREEZE ❄ · V GF OPTION

SUN-DRIED TOMATO SOUP WITH PARMESAN TOAST

You can replace the Parmesan with Cheddar if you have long since given up the battle to introduce Parmesan to your kids.

WHERE ON EARTH: Sun-dried tomatoes can be found next to the pickles and olives, etc.

SOUP

25g **butter** (measure using packet)

2 **red onions**, chopped

3 sticks **celery**, chopped

2 cloves **garlic**, chopped

425g tin **butter beans**, rinsed and drained

½ x 290g jar **sun-dried tomatoes**, chopped

3 mugs (900ml) **water**

2 **vegetable stock cubes** (GF option)

1 teaspoon freshly-chopped **rosemary** leaves or
½ teaspoon **dried rosemary**

PARMESAN TOAST

6 slices **wholemeal bread** (GF option)

butter

1 mug (60g) grated **Parmesan**

1 Heat the butter in a large saucepan. Add the onions and celery and fry until they begin to brown.

2 Add the rest of the soup ingredients and bring to the boil. Season well and simmer for 10 minutes.

3 Meanwhile, lightly toast the bread. Butter it and put the grated Parmesan on the top. Place under the grill until the cheese begins to bubble.

4 Once the soup is cooked, blitz with a hand-held blender, or put in the food-processor. It does not need to be really smooth; leave it a bit rustic.

PETER & BERNICE: "My family HATE butter beans, but they loved this soup. I love that it includes a cheap vegetarian source of protein in an innovative way. The strong flavour of the sun-dried tomatoes makes this soup much more exciting than a regular tomato soup. It tastes creamy without adding any cream! Crispy Parmesan toast contrasts beautifully with the smooth soup."

£0.47 /PERSON · SERVES 4 · EASE ★★★☆☆ · PREP 20 MINS · OK TO FREEZE · V GF OPTION

SPICY BUTTERNUT SQUASH SOUP

1 tablespoon **olive oil**

1 **onion**, sliced

1kg **butternut squash**, peeled and cut into chunks

½ mug (125g) **red lentils**

3 mugs (900ml) **water**

2 **veg stock cubes** (GF option)

1 dessertspoon **Korma curry paste** (GF option) (optional)

1 Heat the oil in a large saucepan and fry the onions and squash until they begin to brown.

2 Add the lentils, water, stock and curry paste. Season well and bring to the boil. Turn down to simmer for 15 minutes. The squash and the lentils should be tender by then.

3 Blitz with a hand-held blender, or food processor.

4 Serve with some crusty bread and cheese.

£1.08 /PERSON | SERVES 4 | EASE ★★★★☆ | PREP 10 MINS | COOK 20 MINS | V GF OPTION

MOZZARELLA STUFFED TOMATOES

4 **large beef tomatoes**

125g **mozzarella cheese**, chopped

1 tablespoon freshly chopped **basil**

2 **ready-roasted red peppers**, roughly chopped

1 tablespoon **red pesto**

4 slices **crusty bread** (GF option)

1 Preheat the oven to 180°C fan/200°C/gas 6. Grease a baking tray.

2 Cut the top off the tomatoes and keep for later. Scoop out the fleshy middles of the tomatoes with a spoon (you can save them for spag bol).

3 Mix the cheese, basil, peppers and pesto together and pile it into the tomatoes. Put the tops back on and place on the greased tray.

4 Place in the oven for 20 minutes.

5 Meanwhile, toast and butter the bread.

6 Once the tomatoes are cooked, place one on each slice of bread and pour over any juice which may have escaped.

MUSHROOM OMELETTE WITH APPLE AND FENNEL SALAD

You can replace the mushrooms with things like tomatoes, small roast potatoes, ham, tuna, prawns, etc. This recipe just gives the basic idea for an omelette.

SALAD

1 **Little Gem lettuce**, finely sliced

3 **spring onions**, chopped

½ bulb **fennel**, finely sliced

1 **red apple**, cored and finely sliced

2 sticks **celery**, finely sliced

8cm piece **cucumber**, cut into thin strips

DRESSING

salt and **pepper**

2 tablespoons **extra virgin olive oil**

juice of a **lemon**

1 teaspoon **granulated sugar**

1 tablespoon **olive oil**

300g **mushrooms**, sliced

6 **spring onions**, chopped

¼ mug (75ml) **water**

1 tablespoon freshly chopped **basil**

6 **eggs**, beaten

2/3 mug (50g) grated **Cheddar cheese**

1 Prepare the salad by mixing the ingredients in a bowl. Mix the dressing ingredients and pour over.

2 Put the grill on a high heat.

3 Heat the oil in a large frying pan. Add the mushrooms and spring onions and fry on a high heat, until the mushrooms begin to brown. Season well with salt and pepper.

4 Mix together the water, basil and eggs and beat. Pour into the frying pan. Allow the egg mixture on the bottom of the pan to set, then gently push around to allow the unset mixture to get to the bottom of the pan. Do this one more time.

5 While there is still a little runny egg in the pan, sprinkle the cheese evenly over the top.

6 Place under the hot grill for 3–4 minutes, until the cheese bubbles and browns. Serve with the salad.

WATCH A VIDEO OF MAKING OMELETTES AT
NOSHBOOKS.COM/OMELETTE

HOISIN AND SESAME TUNA NOODLES

This is essentially a 'one-pot' dish too, so not too heavy on the washing up.

2 tablespoons **toasted sesame oil**

8 **spring onions**, chopped

1 clove **garlic**, finely chopped

6 **mushrooms**, sliced

4 medium **tomatoes**, cut into chunks

2 tablespoons **soy sauce** (GF option)

1 tablespoon **honey**

½ mug (150ml) **water**

1 tablespoon **hoisin sauce** (GF option)

2 x 150g packets **ready-to-wok noodles**

2 x 160g tins **tuna**, drained

1   Heat the oil in a wok and fry the onions and garlic for 30 seconds.

2   Add the mushrooms and tomatoes and fry for a further 30 seconds.

3   Mix together the soy, honey, water and hoisin. Add to the wok. Cook for 30 seconds.

4   Add the noodles and tuna and heat through for no more than 30 seconds. Stir as little as possible, so the tuna does not go mushy.

BEN & NICOLE: "Ridiculously simple. I didn't know I could cook a whole meal in such a short space of time."

EVERYDAY FAST FOOD

You come home from work, or at the end of a busy day looking after the children and you want something uncomplicated. You also don't want the same old thing over and over again. Some of these recipes take minutes to prepare and then cook in the oven for a while. All in all, they won't take much of your precious time.

APPLE AND COCONUT SWEET CURRY

This is a lovely, mild, sweet curry, ideal for younger children who don't want too much spice. You can up the quantity of curry paste, or use hotter curry paste, such as Madras, if you prefer a stronger taste.

basmati rice to serve

1 tablespoon **olive oil**

1 **onion**, chopped

3 **chicken breasts**, cut into bite-sized pieces

2 tablespoons **Korma curry paste** (GF option)

400ml tin **coconut milk**

1 **chicken stock cube** (GF option)

8 **mushrooms**, sliced

2 large **tomatoes**, chopped

1 **red apple**, cut into small chunks

½ mug (100g) **raisins**

1 Put the rice on to cook, see p20.

2 Heat the oil in a wok. Add the onions and fry until they begin to soften. Add the chicken and cook until no longer pink. Add the Korma paste and cook for 30 seconds.

3 Add the coconut milk and stock.

4 Add the mushrooms, tomatoes, apple and raisins and cook for 1 minute. Bring to the boil, then turn down to simmer for 5–6 minutes. Season with salt and pepper.

5 Serve together with the cooked rice.

GARY & NIKKI: "My kids don't usually like curry, but they liked this one."

WATCH A VIDEO OF HOW TO MAKE PERFECT RICE AT
NOSHBOOKS.COM/RICE

MOROCCAN HONEY CHICKEN

Depending on your family, or your own taste, you can add the juice of half the lemon to the couscous, along with the rind, if you want to add a little extra kick.

1 mug **couscous**

zest of a **lemon**

2 mugs (600ml) **boiling water**

1 **chicken stock cube**

1 tablespoon **olive oil**

1 **onion**, sliced

1 clove **garlic**, finely chopped

1 **red pepper**, cut into small chunks

3 **chicken breasts**, cut into bite-sized pieces

400g tin **chickpeas**, rinsed and drained

1 teaspoon **ground cumin**

1 teaspoon **ground coriander**

1¹/₂ tablespoons **honey**

1 teaspoon **cinnamon**

¹/₄ teaspoon **chilli powder** (optional)

400g tin **chopped tomatoes**

1 Put the couscous in a bowl with the lemon zest. Add the boiling water and the stock. Stir once. Put a plate over the bowl and leave to absorb all of the water. This should take 4–5 minutes.

2 Heat the oil in a large saucepan or wok. Add the onions, garlic and peppers and fry until they begin to soften.

3 Add the chicken and season with salt and pepper. Cook until the chicken is no longer pink.

4 Add the rest of the ingredients (excluding the couscous) and bring to the boil. Turn down to simmer for 5–6 minutes.

5 Serve as seen in the photo opposite.

CREAMY CHICKEN AND MUSHROOM PIE

If your shallow casserole dish does not have a lid, just use some foil.

ONE MORE THING: A great way to do your carrots is to bake them in the oven in a covered dish. Do this before you start preparing your chicken pie, so they should be ready by the time your pie is finished. Just bake them with a little water, butter, salt and pepper. You can even drizzle over some honey, just before serving, to make them even tastier.

4 large **potatoes**, cut into small chunks

50g **butter** (measured using packet)

300g pack **cream cheese with garlic & herbs**

300ml **double cream**

1 **chicken stock cube** (GF option)

3 **chicken breasts**, cut into bite-sized pieces

6 **spring onions**, chopped

8 **mushrooms**, sliced

1 mug (150g) defrosted **frozen peas**

6–8 medium **carrots**, sliced

1   Preheat the oven to 180°C fan/200°C/gas 6. Grease a large, shallow, casserole dish with oil.

2   Half-fill a saucepan with boiling water, add the cubed potatoes and season with salt. Bring back to the boil, then turn down to simmer for 10 minutes. Drain and add the butter, allowing it to melt. Put a lid on the pan and shake the potatoes to distribute the butter evenly.

3   Mix the cream cheese and the cream together in a bowl until smooth. Add the chicken stock and season with salt and pepper.

4   Add the chicken, onions, mushrooms and peas into a shallow casserole dish and mix together. Pour into a casserole dish.

5   Pour the creamy mix over the top.

6   Put the potatoes on top. Place in the oven for 20 minutes with a lid on and for a further 25–30 minutes with the lid off, until the potatoes are browned.

7   Meanwhile, put the carrots in a saucepan of boiling, salted water. Simmer for 5 minutes. Drain and serve with the pie.

BEN & NICOLE: "Bella loved this, Toby did eat some, but he is being generally picky at the moment."

£2.05 /PERSON · SERVES 4 · EASE ★★★☆☆ · PREP 30 MINS · OK TO FREEZE ❄ · GF OPTION

FENNEL CHICKEN PASTA

Some younger children may find the taste of the fennel seeds a bit strange. You could just leave them out, as there are plenty of other tasty ingredients.

250g **tagliatelli** or **spaghetti** (GF option)

3 **chicken breasts**

½ mug (100g) **pine nuts**

½ teaspoon **fennel seeds**

1 tablespoon **olive oil**

1 **red onion**, chopped

1 clove **garlic**, finely chopped

5 **tomatoes**, chopped

5 **sun-dried tomatoes**, chopped

juice of a **lemon**

1 teaspoon **granulated sugar**

1 Cook the pasta, see p21, drain and set to one side.

2 Half fill a medium pan with boiling water, put the 3 chicken breasts in the water and bring back to the boil. Turn the heat off, put a lid on the pan and leave for 15 minutes. After that time, choose the largest piece and check that it is cooked through. If not, bring back to the boil again and leave to stand for 5 minutes. Cut into bite-sized pieces.

3 Put the pine nuts and fennel seeds in a dry frying pan and toast for about 1 minute, until the pine nuts begin to brown. Shake the pan to move the nuts around. Take out of the pan and leave until needed.

4 Heat the oil in the frying pan and fry the onions and garlic until the onions become soft. Add the tomatoes and the sun-dried tomatoes and fry for 2–3 minutes until the tomatoes begin to lose their shape. Add the lemon juice, nuts, fennel seeds and the sugar and heat through. Season well.

5 Add the chicken to the tomato mixture and spoon over the pasta. Serve.

JOE & SARAH: "Nice and light, good for the summer and easy too."

HONEY CHICKEN BAKE

If you ever have some dry bread that you would normally throw away, why not make it into breadcrumbs and put it in the freezer for a later date.

3 **chicken breasts**, cut into bite-sized pieces

1½ tablespoons **honey**

1½ tablespoons **soy sauce** (GF option)

1 tablespoon **olive oil**

2 **onions**, sliced

1 clove **garlic**, finely chopped

2 medium **courgettes**, cut into small pieces

6 **mushrooms**, sliced

1 teaspoon **dried mixed herbs**

4 **tomatoes**, chopped

12 **olives**, halved (optional)

4 slices **bread** (GF option), made into breadcrumbs

1 mug (75g) grated **Cheddar cheese**

1 Put the chicken in a bowl and add the honey and soy. Mix together and leave until needed.

2 Heat the oil in a frying pan and fry the onions and garlic until they begin to soften. Add the courgettes, mushrooms and mixed herbs. Fry on a medium heat for 5 minutes.

3 Add the chicken and the juices and cook for 2–3 minutes.

4 Add the tomatoes and olives and season well. Cook on a high heat for 2 minutes. Pour everything into a casserole dish.

5 Mix the breadcrumbs and cheese together and sprinkle evenly over the casserole dish.

6 Place under a grill for 5–10 minutes until the cheese is browned.

ADAM & CONNIE: "Very appealing, full of flavour and fairly cheap to make. Really good way of getting vegetables into the kids".

£ 1.13 /PERSON · SERVES 6 · EASE ★★★☆☆ · PREP 30 MINS · COOK 35 MINS · OK TO FREEZE

CHICKEN AND ROAST VEGETABLE COUSCOUS

Any leftovers here can be frozen and used for lunch boxes, as it doesn't need to be hot to be yummy. You can also serve this cold with salad.

2 large **sweet potatoes**, peeled and cut into small chunks

2 **courgettes**, chopped

4 large **tomatoes**, roughly chopped

6 **mushrooms**, sliced

2 **onions**, chopped

1 teaspoon **ground cumin**

1 teaspoon **ground coriander**

1 teaspoon **ground cinnamon**

4 tablespoons **olive oil**

1 mug (200g) **couscous**

2 mugs (600ml) **boiling water**

2 **chicken stock cubes**

2 tablespoons **sun-dried tomato purée** (can use normal tomato purée)

1 tablespoon **olive oil**

3 **chicken breasts**

1 Preheat the oven to 200°C fan/220°C/gas 7.

2 Place all the vegetables on a large baking tray with the spices and the oil. Use your hands to spread everything evenly. Season with salt and pepper. Cook in the oven for 30–35 minutes until the vegetables are browned.

3 Place the couscous in a large bowl and add the water, chicken stock and tomato purée. Stir well. Cover and leave until needed.

4 Heat the oil in a frying pan and pan roast the chicken breast. Cook on a high heat for 2 minutes each side. Turn down the heat, cover the pan with a lid or foil and cook for 4 minutes each side. Cut or tear into small pieces and add on top of the couscous.

5 Mix the cooked vegetables and any juices to the couscous and serve.

BEN & NICOLE: "This is one of our favourite easy-to-cook meals."

WATCH A VIDEO OF PAN ROASTING CHICKEN AT
NOSHBOOKS.COM/PAN-CHICKEN

COCONUT POACHED THAI CHICKEN

LEE & SARAH: "Good basis for a family to try, not being too hot and able to add more zing next time you cook it. This was a real hit with all. Yum!"

1½ mugs (375g) **basmati rice**

1 **chicken stock cube** (GF option)

1 tablespoon freshly grated **ginger**

3 **chicken breasts**, cut into bite-sized pieces

1 tablespoon **Thai red curry paste** (GF option) (add extra if your kids are happy with spice)

400ml tin **coconut milk**

6 **spring onions**, chopped

1 tablespoon **fish sauce**

6 **mushrooms**, sliced

juice of a **lime**

1 dessertspoon **cornflour** mixed with 2 tablespoons of water

2 tablespoons freshly chopped **coriander**

1　Put the rice on to cook, see p20.

2　Put everything but the coriander and cornflour into a saucepan or wok and bring to the boil. Simmer gently for 10 minutes.

3　Add the cornflour and water and stir until the sauce thickens. Stir in the coriander and serve.

 £1.34 /PERSON   SERVES 4   EASE ★★☆☆☆   PREP 20 MINS   COOK 25 MINS   OK TO FREEZE ❄   GF OPTION

BACON AND MOZZARELLA PASTA BAKE

2 mugs (200g) **pasta** (we used penne) (GF option)

1 tablespoon **olive oil**

300g pack **smoked streaky bacon**

4 **sun-dried tomatoes**, chopped

6 medium-sized **tomatoes**, roughly chopped

300ml **double cream**

250g **mozzarella**

1 slice **wholemeal bread** (GF option), made into breadcrumbs

1 tablespoon freshly chopped **basil**

1 Preheat the oven to 180°C fan/200°C/gas 6.

2 Cook the pasta, drain and leave until needed.

3 Heat the oil in a frying pan and fry the bacon until it is crispy and then chop into small pieces.

4 Mix the bacon, sun-dried tomatoes, tomatoes and cream into the pasta and mix well. Season with pepper (the bacon will have enough salt). Pour into the casserole dish.

5 Pull apart the mozzarella and place over the pasta mix. Sprinkle the breadcrumbs over the top and place in the oven for 25 minutes until the cheese begins to brown.

6 Sprinkle the chopped basil over the top.

CHORIZO AND PANCETTA BAKE

This is a complete meal in one dish. Really easy to do and lots of different textures and flavours to makes it unusual and interesting.

WHERE ON EARTH: Pancetta lardons can be found next to the cooked meats in the supermarket. Make sure you get pancetta lardons and not normal bacon lardons.

2 tablespoons **olive oil**

100g **pancetta lardons**

4 small **chorizo sausages** (GF option), sliced

1 **onion**, sliced

1 **red** or **yellow pepper**, chopped

2 cloves **garlic**, finely chopped

¼ mug (75ml) **water**

6 **mushrooms**, sliced

1 tablespoon **tomato purée**

400g tin **chopped tomatoes**

3 tablespoons freshly chopped **parsley**

6–8 **eggs**

2 slices **wholemeal bread** (GF option), buttered and cut into small squares

1 Preheat the oven to 180°C fan/200°C/gas 6. Grease a large casserole dish.

2 Heat a little oil in a wok and fry the pancetta and chorizo until they begin to brown. Take out and set to one side.

3 Add the onions, peppers and garlic to the pan and fry until they begin to brown.

4 Add the water, mushrooms, tomato purée and chopped tomatoes. Simmer for 5–6 minutes.

5 Return the pancetta and chorizo to the pan and add the parsley. Stir in.

6 Pour into the casserole dish. Make small hollows in the mixture and break the eggs into each. Sprinkle the cubed bread over the top and place in the oven for 25–30 minutes. The eggs should be cooked and the bread crisp.

£1.25 /PERSON · SERVES 4 · EASE ★★★☆☆ · PREP 25 MINS · COOK 55 MINS · OK TO FREEZE ❄

BEEF AND POTATO HOT-POT

This is similar to our 'Monday Pie' from 'Nosh for Students', but we have included it in this book, as it is just perfect for families too.

ONE MORE THING: If you have a hob-to-oven casserole dish, this is a great one-pot dish. Easy to prepare and then just leave it in the oven to do its thing.

ACTUALLY…ONE MORE THING: You can use a food processor to slice the potatoes, it saves time and makes them nice and thin.

---

1 tablespoon **olive oil**

1 **onion**, sliced

750g **minced beef**

1 **beef stock cube**

½ mug (150ml) **water**

400g tin **baked beans**

4 **tomatoes**, chopped

1 tablespoon **tomato purée**

1 tablespoon **Worcestershire sauce**

5 large **potatoes**, thinly sliced

green veg to serve

1 Preheat the oven to 180°C fan/200°C/gas 6.

2 Heat the oil in a hob-to-oven casserole, or wok, and fry the onion until it becomes soft.

3 Add the mince and fry until no longer pink.

4 Add the stock, water, beans, tomatoes, tomato purée and Worcestershire sauce. Heat through and season well. Leave in the hob-to-oven casserole or transfer to a large, greased casserole dish.

5 Arrange the sliced potatoes evenly over the top of the meat mixture. Season well with salt and pepper.

6 Put the lid on the casserole and place in the oven for 30 minutes. Take the lid off and cook for a further 25 minutes. The potatoes should be browned.

7 Serve with green veg.

LEMON COUSCOUS SALAD

Good one to freeze in portions for lunch boxes. If you take them out in the morning, they will be defrosted by lunch-time.

ONE MORE THING: This works best with fresh herbs. Try not to use freeze-dried ones.

1½ mugs (300g) **couscous**

3 mugs (900ml) **water**

1 **chicken stock cube**

DRESSING

4 tablespoons **extra virgin olive oil**

juice and zest of a **lemon**

1 tablespoon freshly chopped **coriander**

1 tablespoon freshly chopped **basil**

salt and **pepper**

¼ teaspoon **cumin**

¼ teaspoon **cayenne pepper**

1 tablespoon **olive oil**

1 **onion**, chopped

2 **courgettes**, chopped

3 **chicken breasts**, cut into bite-sized chunks

6 **mushrooms**, sliced

3 **tomatoes**, chopped

12–16 **black olives**

1 Place the couscous in a bowl and add 3 mugs of boiling water and the stock. Cover with a plate and leave to stand for 5 minutes until all the water is absorbed.

2 Mix together the dressing ingredients and leave to stand.

3 Heat the oil in a frying pan and fry the onions and courgettes until they become soft.

4 Add the chicken and mushrooms. Fry until the chicken is no longer pink.

5 Add the tomatoes, olives and dressing and mix together.

6 Mix together with the couscous.

GINGER CHICKEN STIR-FRY

Omit the chilli, or add less, if you have younger children who don't like spice.

WHERE ON EARTH: Sesame oil is usually found with the other oils. Straight-to-wok noodles can be found in the 'world food section'. If you want to use fresh noodles, they are kept in the 'salad section'.

¼ mug (75ml) **water**

2 tablespoons **white wine vinegar**

6 **spring onions**, sliced

2 tablespoons **honey**

2 tablespoons **soy sauce** (GF option)

1 tablespoon freshly grated **ginger**

1 **fat red chilli**, deseeded and finely chopped

1 teaspoon **cornflour**

2 tablespoons **toasted sesame oil**

3 **chicken breasts**, cut into strips

2 **yellow** or **red peppers**, cut into small bite-sized strips

5 **mushrooms**, sliced

400g pack **straight-to-wok noodles** (GF option: use **rice noodles**)

1 tablespoon freshly chopped **coriander**

1 In a medium bowl, stir together the water, vinegar, spring onions, honey, soy sauce, ginger, chilli and cornflour.

2 Heat the sesame oil in a wok and add the chicken. Fry until it is no longer pink. Add the peppers and mushrooms and fry for a minute.

3 Add the onion mixture and heat through. Add the noodles and heat through. Sprinkle over with chopped coriander and serve.

BEN & NICOLE: "Although there were lots of ingredients that would normally have put me off cooking it, it was really worth the extra effort. I really enjoyed cooking it and felt like it made me a better cook. Oh my! Did it taste good!"

CHICKEN TETRAZZINI

Poaching is a great way to cook chicken, it is really easy and keeps the chicken lovely and tender. If, when you come to cut it, it is not cooked through, simply put back in the water and bring to the boil again and then it should be fine.

2 **chicken breasts**

1 head **broccoli**

2½ mugs (200g) **pasta** (we used conchiglie) (GF option)

2 **carrots**, thinly sliced

75g **butter** (measure using packet)

2 tablespoons **flour** (GF option)

2 mugs (600ml) **milk**

¼ mug (75ml) **double cream**

1 **chicken stock cube** (GF option)

1 tablespoon freshly chopped **basil**, or 1 teaspoon **dried basil**

1 mug (75g) grated **Cheddar cheese**

½ mug (100g) **pine nuts**

1 Grease a large casserole dish.

2 Fill a small pan with boiling water, add the chicken breasts and bring back to the boil. Turn the heat off and put a lid on the pan. Leave for 15 minutes.

3 Cut the very tops off the broccoli and chop the stem into small pieces.

4 Put the pasta on to cook with the stem of the broccoli and the sliced carrots. Cook for 5 minutes. Add the broccoli heads and cook for a further 5 minutes. Drain everything and return to the pan.

5 To make the sauce, melt the butter in a pan and add the flour. Mix together. Add the milk, cream and stock and gently bring to the boil, stirring all the time. The sauce should thicken. Season well and add the basil.

6 Cut the cooked chicken into bite-sized pieces. Mix the chicken, pasta and vegetables with the sauce and pour into the casserole dish.

7 Mix the cheese and pine nuts together and sprinkle over the casserole. Place under a hot grill until the cheese is browned.

WATCH A VIDEO OF MAKING A ROUX SAUCE
NOSHBOOKS.COM/ROUX

CREAMY TOMATO CHICKEN

250g **spaghetti** or **tagliatelli** (GF option)

1 tablespoon **olive oil**

1 small **onion**, chopped

1 clove **garlic**, finely chopped

2 large **chicken breasts**, cut into thin strips

8 **mushrooms**, sliced

3 **tomatoes**, chopped

½ mug (150ml) **double cream**

½ **chicken stock cube** (GF option)

1 tablespoon **tomato purée**

2 tablespoons freshly chopped **basil**

1 Put the spaghetti on to cook, see p21.

2 Heat the oil in a frying pan and fry the onion and garlic until the onion begins to soften.

3 Add the chicken and fry until no longer pink.

4 Add the mushrooms and tomato. Fry for 1–2 minutes.

5 Add the cream, stock, tomato purée and season with salt and pepper. Bring to boil and then turn down to simmer for 2 minutes.

6 Serve with the pasta and basil.

CRISPY FRIED LAMB

4 **potatoes**

500g **lamb mince**

1 **red onion**, sliced

1 clove **garlic**, chopped

2 medium **carrots**, coarsely grated (in a processor if you have one)

2 medium **courgettes**, chopped

2 tablespoons **balsamic vinegar**

½ mug (150ml) **water**

1 **lamb** or **vegetable stock cube** (GF option)

1 dessertspoon **honey**

1 tablespoon freshly chopped **mint**, or 1 teaspoon **dried mint**

1 Preheat the oven to 180°C fan/200°C/gas 6. Put the potatoes on a tray and bake for 50 minutes.

2 Heat a large frying pan. Add the lamb mince and cook on a fairly high heat until it is browned and crispy. Stir frequently.

3 Add the onion, garlic, carrots and courgettes and cook until the onions begin to soften.

4 Add the vinegar, water and stock cube. Put a lid over (or foil) and simmer gently for 5 minutes, or until the carrot is tender. Add more water if things get dry.

5 Take off the heat and add the honey and mint. Stir and season well with salt and pepper.

6 Serve with the baked potatoes.

£ 1.62 /PERSON · SERVES 4 · EASE ★★★☆☆ · PREP 35 MINS · OK TO FREEZE · GF OPTION

ONE-POT CHICKEN KORMA

If you like things spicy, you can add an extra tablespoon of curry paste, or use a hotter paste like Madras.

ONE MORE THING: Minimal washing up with this one as you only have to use one pot.

---

1 tablespoon **olive oil**

2 **onions**, sliced

2 cloves **garlic**, finely chopped

2 **chicken breasts**, cut into bite-sized pieces

1 tablespoon **Korma curry paste** (GF option)

4 **tomatoes**, chopped

1 mug (250g) **basmati rice**

2 mugs (600ml) **water**

1 **chicken stock cube** (GF option)

1/2 mug (100g) **raisins**

1/4 mug (50g) **pine nuts**

100g **fresh spinach**

crème fraîche or **Greek yogurt**, to serve

1 Heat the oil in a wok. Add the onions and garlic and fry until soft.

2 Add the chicken pieces and cook until no longer pink.

3 Add the curry paste and tomatoes. Fry for 30 seconds.

4 Add the rice and cook for a further 30 seconds.

5 Add the water, stock and raisins. Bring to the boil.

6 Cover with a lid or foil. Turn down to simmer for 10–15 minutes, until most of the water has been absorbed.

7 Add the pine nuts and the fresh spinach. Stir until the spinach is wilted, this should only take 30 seconds or so.

8 Serve with a little yogurt.

JO: "Was not sure the kids would like this but they ate the lot! I have never given them spinach before, Ollie admitted it was OK. We have never eaten pine nuts before, but we liked the texture they gave."

BALSAMIC CHILLI BEEF RAGU

This is a bit of a spin on the classic 'spag bol'. It has a few more ingredients and a slightly richer flavour.

ONE MORE THING: If you don't have a food processor, just finely chop the carrots, celery, onion and chilli.

---

2 medium **carrots**, peeled

3 sticks **celery**

1 **onion**, peeled and quartered

1 **fat red chilli**, finely chopped

1 clove **garlic**, finely chopped

1 tablespoon **olive oil**

500g **minced beef**

3 tablespoons **balsamic vinegar**

400g tin **chopped tomatoes**

1 tablespoon **tomato purée**

1 mug (300ml) **water**

1 **beef stock cube** (GF option)

1 teaspoon **granulated sugar**

2 mugs (200g) **pasta** (we used fusilli) (GF option)

1 tablespoon freshly chopped **basil**

Parmesan cheese (optional)

1 Put the carrots, celery, onion, chilli and garlic in a food processor and blitz.

2 Heat the oil in a large pan and add the vegetables, cooking for 3–4 minutes.

3 Add the mince to the pan and cook until no longer pink. Add the balsamic vinegar and cook for 1 minute.

4 Add the tomatoes, tomato purée, water, stock and sugar. Bring to the boil and then leave to simmer for 10 minutes.

5 Meanwhile, cook the pasta, see p21. Once cooked, drain, but retain some of the cooking liquid.

6 Add the pasta to the meat sauce and stir well. If necessary, add some of the pasta water. The sauce should be quite wet. Add the fresh basil and stir in.

7 To serve, grate a little Parmesan over the top.

CRUNCHY TOPPED TUNA BAKE

This is a bit of a posh tuna bake. However, it is still inexpensive. The crispy topping is a winner with the kids too.

2 mugs (200g) **pasta** (we used fusilli) (GF option)

50g **butter** (measure on packet)

2 heaped tablespoons **flour** (GF option)

2 mugs (600ml) **milk**

1 mug (75g) grated **Cheddar cheese**

2 x 160g tins **tuna**, drained

½ x 300g pack **mushrooms**, sliced

125g **cherry tomatoes**, halved

½ mug (40g) grated **Cheddar cheese**

2 slices **wholemeal bread** (GF option), made into breadcrumbs

green salad to serve

1 Preheat the oven to 180°C fan/200°C/gas 6. Lightly grease a large casserole dish.

2 Cook the pasta, drain and leave until needed.

3 To make the cheese sauce, put the butter in a saucepan and gently melt. Add the flour, stir well and cook for 30 seconds. Add the milk and stir well. Bring to the boil, stirring frequently (a small whisk works well for this). Add the cheese. The sauce should thicken. Season well.

4 Put the tuna, mushrooms, tomato and pasta in the bottom of the casserole dish. Gently fold things around a bit, but don't stir, as the tuna will go mushy. Season well with pepper and a little salt to taste.

5 Pour the cheese sauce evenly over the top. Sprinkle over with the grated cheese and breadcrumbs.

6 Place in the oven for 25 minutes until the top is nicely browned.

7 Serve with a green salad.

PETER & BERNICE: "Nice, tasty and easy recipe. Everyone liked it."

WATCH A VIDEO OF MAKING A ROUX SAUCE AT
NOSHBOOKS.COM/ROUX

SOMETHING FOR THE WEEKEND

Weekends are times to relax and not rush
around so much. Lots of the recipes here
need time to cook in the oven, but you
will end up with some delicious food. I
have also included some breakfast ideas
for those relaxed Saturday and Sunday
mornings when you don't have work, or
have the school-run to contend with. Ideal
for getting the kids involved.

SIMPLE SATURDAY BRUNCH

This is great for chilling out on a Saturday morning when everyone has got up a little late. Cooking the sausages and bacon in the oven avoids you having to stand around too many frying pans in your pyjamas and smelling like a 'greasy spoon cafe' when you go to bed later that day!

4 **sausages** (GF option)

8 rashers **bacon**

2 **eggs**, beaten

4 slices **bread** (GF option)

1 tablespoon **olive oil**

400g tin **baked beans**

1 Preheat the oven to 180°C fan/200°C/gas 6. Grease 2 baking trays.

2 Place the sausages on one tray and place in the oven for 40 minutes.

3 10 minutes into the cooking time, place the bacon on the other tray and place in the oven. Cook for the remaining 30 minutes.

4 About 10 minutes before the end of the cooking time for the sausages, place the beaten eggs on a large plate and season well. Dip both sides of each slice of bread in the egg mixture. Make sure each side is completely covered in egg.

5 Heat the oil in a frying pan. Add the bread and cook for 1–2 minutes, each side, until the egg is browned.

6 Serve with the sausages, bacon and cooked beans.

£ 0.81 /PERSON

SERVES 4

EASE ★★☆☆☆

PREP 30 MINS

GF OPTION

AMERICAN BREAKFAST PANCAKES

Poaching eggs is easy if you have gently simmering water in the frying pan. See video link below.

1½ mugs (300g) **self-raising flour** (GF option)

¼ mug (65g) **granulated sugar**

4 **eggs**

½ mug (150ml) **milk**

Trex to fry

8 rashers **bacon**

4 **eggs**

maple syrup to serve

1 Put the flour, sugar, eggs and milk in a bowl and mix well, or put everything in a food processor. It should be thicker than a normal pancake mix.

2 Heat a little Trex in a frying pan. Once hot, add the pancake mix, 3 tablespoons at a time, in order to make small pancakes. No need to spread out the mixture. Cook one at a time. This mixture should make 6 pancakes.

3 Keep the pancakes warm on a plate with some foil over the top. Fry or grill the bacon until crispy.

4 Meanwhile, poach the eggs. Put some boiling water into a large frying pan and bring to simmering point. Break an egg into a cup, lower into the boiling water and gently pour out. Repeat the process with each egg. You may find it necessary to spoon over the yoke with some of the boiling water to fully cook the egg. Simmer until the white of the egg is fully cooked.

5 Serve with the maple syrup and crispy bacon.

BEN & NICOLE: "We like to do this for special breakfasts every now and then. Don't knock the maple syrup and bacon 'til you try it. One of my best food discoveries of the year."

WATCH A VIDEO OF POACHING EGGS AT
NOSHBOOKS.COM/POACHING-EGGS

EGG-FRIED PLOUGHMAN'S

8 slices **bread**, buttered (GF option)

1½ mugs (110g) grated **Cheddar cheese**

pickles or sliced **tomatoes**

4 **eggs**, beaten and seasoned with **salt** and **pepper**

25g **butter** (measure using packet)

1 Preheat the oven to 160°C fan/180°C/gas 5.

2 Make up the sandwiches with the cheese and either the sliced tomatoes or the pickle.

3 Pour ½ the beaten eggs onto a large plate and dip 2 of the sandwiches into the egg, allowing the egg to soak up a little on each side. Repeat with the rest of the egg and the other two sandwiches.

4 Heat the butter in the pan and fry the sandwiches on a low heat, on each side, until browned. The cheese will also melt in the middle. Repeat with all the sandwiches, storing them in the preheated oven to keep warm.

5 Serve with a little salad.

£ 0.61 /PERSON · SERVES 4 · EASE ★★★☆☆ · PREP 30 MINS · V GF OPTION

BLUEBERRY PANCAKES WITH CARAMEL SAUCE

CARAMEL SAUCE

100g **butter** (measure using packet)

4 tablespoons **brown sugar**

1/2 mug (150ml) **double cream**

3 **eggs**

1/4 mug (65g) **granulated sugar**

1 1/4 mugs (250g) **self-raising flour** (GF option)

1/4 mug (75ml) **milk**

1/4 x 400g packet defrosted **frozen blueberries**

Trex to fry

1 Put the sauce ingredients in a small saucepan and bringing to the boil. Simmer for 30 seconds and then set to one side until needed.

2 Beat the eggs, sugar and flour together and then add the milk to make a thick creamy consistency.

3 Drain the blueberries and add just before you begin to cook the pancakes.

4 Heat a little Trex in a frying pan. Add about a tablespoon of the pancake mix and allow it to spread in the pan. You should get three in the pan at one time. Cook on a medium heat. Leave to cook on one side and then flip over to lightly brown the other side. Repeat until all the pancakes are cooked.

5 Serve with the caramel sauce, or maple syrup.

SALMON CAKES WITH HOISIN DIP

You can freeze the salmon cakes before you cook them, then defrost and fry them when you need them.

ONE MORE THING: You could add a chopped red chilli to the sauce if you like your food spicy.

2 large **potatoes**, peeled and cut into chunks

400g **salmon fillet**

DIPPING SAUCE

1 tablespoon **olive oil**

2 **spring onions**, chopped

2 tablespoons **hoisin sauce** (GF option)

1 teaspoon **soy sauce** (GF option)

2 teaspoons **cornflour**

1 teaspoon **granulated sugar**

1 tablespoon **olive oil**

3 **spring onions**, chopped

½ x 340g tin **sweetcorn**

1 **egg yolk**

2 tablespoons **flour** (GF option)

2 **eggs**, beaten

3 slices **wholemeal bread**, made into breadcrumbs (GF option)

1 tablespoon **olive oil**

bag of **salad**

1 Add the potatoes to boiling, salted water, and simmer for 10 minutes. 5 minutes before the end of the cooking time, add the salmon fillet to the pan.

2 Meanwhile, make the sauce. Heat the oil in a small saucepan, add the 2 spring onions and fry for 1 minute. Mix together the rest of the sauce ingredients in a mug. Add enough water to make one mug of liquid and then add to the pan. Bring to the boil, the sauce should thicken.

3 Once the potatoes and the salmon are cooked, drain. Take out the salmon, remove the skin and flake the fish into a bowl. Mash the potatoes and stir in the fish.

4 Heat the oil in a frying pan and fry the 3 spring onions for 1–2 minutes until they begin to soften.

5 Add the onions to the potatoes and fish, along with the sweetcorn and egg yolk. Season well with salt and pepper. Mix together.

6 Form the mixture into 8–10 cakes and place on a floured board.

7 Put the beaten egg in a shallow dish. Dip the formed cakes in the egg and then into the breadcrumbs.

8 Heat the oil in a frying pan and, once hot, add the salmon cakes. You may have to fry in 2 batches. Cook on a medium heat for 2–3 minutes each side, or until the cakes are browned and crispy on the outside.

BARBECUE CHICKEN WITH APPLE SALAD

The salad with this one is a little different. Do give it a try, but if you don't like the combination of potato wedges and salad, it is also great with corn on the cob.

Why not try out some other salads from page see p32.

---

8 **chicken thighs (skin on)**

4 medium **potatoes**, cut into wedges

1 tablespoon **olive oil**

BBQ SAUCE

1 clove **garlic**

3 **sun-dried tomatoes**, chopped + 1 tablespoon of **oil from the jar**

3 tablespoons **soy sauce** (GF option)

2 tablespoons **honey**

1 tablespoon **tomato purée**

salt and **pepper**

SALAD

1 **Little Gem lettuce**

2 sticks **celery**

8cm piece **cucumber**

2 **spring onions**

1/2 **fennel** bulb

1 **red apple**, cored

DRESSING

juice of 1/2 **lemon**

1 tablespoon **extra virgin olive oil**

1 teaspoon **granulated sugar**

1 tablespoon freshly chopped **basil**

salt and **pepper**

1 Preheat the oven to 180°C fan/200°C/gas 6.

2 Put the chicken thighs in a large, greased casserole dish. Put in the oven for 25 minutes.

3 Put the potato wedges on a roasting tray and sprinkle with oil and salt and pepper. Distribute well. Put in the oven for 35–40 minutes.

4 Blitz the BBQ sauce ingredients together in a food processor. After the chicken thighs have been cooked for 25 minutes, take them out of the oven and spread the sauce over them. Return to the oven for a further 25 minutes until browned.

5 Slice the salad ingredients in the food processor, or thinly slice by hand. Add the dressing just before serving.

MOROCCAN LAMB PIE

If you have a hob-to-oven casserole dish, this is a one-pot meal.

4 large **potatoes**, cut into chunks

25g **butter** (measure using packet)

1 tablespoon **olive oil**

1 **onion**, sliced

2 medium **carrots**, cut into chunks

1 teaspoon freshly grated **ginger**

1 clove **garlic**, finely chopped

500g **lamb mince**

1 teaspoon **ground cumin**

1 teaspoon **ground coriander**

½ teaspoon **paprika**

400g tin **chopped tomatoes**

1 **lamb** or **vegetable stock cube** (GF option)

1 mug (300ml) **water**

1 Preheat the oven to 180°C fan/200°C/ gas 6.

2 Put the potatoes in boiling, salted water and simmer for 10 minutes. Drain and return to pan. Add the butter and stir. Crush with a potato masher, but do not completely mash.

3 Heat the oil in a hob-to-oven casserole or large saucepan and add the onion, carrots, ginger and garlic. Fry until the onions begin to soften.

4 Add the mince and fry until it is no longer pink.

5 Add the cumin, coriander and paprika. Cook for 30 seconds.

6 Add the tomatoes, stock and water and bring to the boil. Once boiling, season well. Pour into a casserole dish if you have not used a hob-to-oven casserole.

7 Spread the crushed potatoes over the top of the mince mixture and place in the oven, without a lid, for 30 minutes, until the potatoes are browned a little.

STEVE & CANDY: "Really enjoyed cooking with lamb mince and doing something with it that I have not previously cooked. Great family meal."

SWEET PORK AND APPLE STEW

Good one-pot dish, which includes all the vegetables you will need for a full meal.

2 tablespoons **olive oil**

2 **onions**, sliced

1 **leek**, sliced

4 **carrots**, sliced

2 cloves **garlic**, finely chopped

1kg **diced pork shoulder**

1 tablespoon **flour** (GF option)

2 **Cox's apples**, cored and cut into chunks

1 mug (300ml) **apple juice**

2 tablespoons **cider vinegar**

1 mug (300ml) **water**

2 **vegetable stock cubes** (GF option)

3 sprigs **fresh thyme**, or 1 teaspoon **dried thyme**

4 large **potatoes**, cut into chunks

1 Preheat the oven to 180°C fan/200°C/gas 6.

2 Heat the oil in a hob-to-oven casserole. Add the onions, leeks, carrots and garlic. Fry until they begin to brown.

3 Add the pork and fry until it is no longer pink on the outside.

4 Add the flour and mix well. Add the apples, apple juice, cider vinegar, water, stock and thyme and bring to the boil. The sauce should thicken a little. Season well. Add the fresh thyme.

5 Take off the heat and arrange the cubed potatoes on the top. Season well with salt and pepper.

6 Place in the oven, with the lid on, for 60 minutes. Take the lid off and cook for a further 30–35 minutes until the potatoes are browned.

 £ 1.32 /PERSON
 SERVES 4
 EASE ★★★☆☆
 PREP 30 MINS
 COOK 25 MINS
 OK TO FREEZE ❄
 GF OPTION

BEEF AND BACON BAKE

Great one-pot dish if you have a hob-to-oven casserole dish.

1 tablespoon **olive oil**

8 rashers **streaky bacon**, chopped

1 **red pepper**, chopped

1 **onion**, sliced

2 cloves **garlic**, finely chopped

500g **minced beef**

1 mug (250g) **basmati rice**

1½ mugs (450ml) **water**

6 **tomatoes**, chopped

1 tablespoon **tomato purée**

1 **beef stock cube** (GF option)

1 tablespoon freshly chopped **basil** or 1 teaspoon **dried basil**

1 mug (75g) grated **Cheddar cheese**

1 Preheat the oven to 180°C fan/200°C/gas 6.

2 Heat the oil in a hob-to-oven casserole and add the bacon, peppers, onions and garlic. Fry until they begin to brown.

3 Add the mince and cook until it is no longer pink.

4 Add the rice and cook for 30 seconds.

5 Add the water, tomatoes, tomato purée, stock and basil. Season well. Bring to the boil.

6 Take off the heat and sprinkle the grated cheese over the top. Place in the oven for 20–25 minutes until the cheese is browned.

ANDY & HEATHER: "I really like one-pot dishes, especially when it comes to clearing up. This is an original idea, cooking rice in the dish. It's really tasty."

£ 1.72 /PERSON · SERVES 4 · EASE ★★★★★ · PREP 20 MINS · COOK 30 MINS · GF OPTION

SCRUMPY PORK PIE

No need to cut the edges off the pastry. Just loosely lay it over the top and scrunch it in a little. This way you don't have to faff about with crimping and there is much more pastry to go around.

4 large **potatoes**, cut into chunks

2 tablespoons **olive oil**

1 **onion**, sliced

1 clove **garlic**, finely chopped

2 sticks **celery**, sliced

1 large **sweet potato**, peeled and cut into chunks

500g **pork mince**

2 tablespoons **flour** (GF option)

1 mug (300ml) **cider**

1 **vegetable stock cube** (GF option)

1 teaspoon **dried thyme**, or 3–4 **fresh sprigs**

½ mug (150ml) **water**

1 sheet **ready-rolled puff pastry** (GF option)

1 beaten **egg**

green veg to serve

1 Preheat the oven to 200°C fan/220°C/gas 7.

2 Put the potatoes on a baking tray and sprinkle a tablespoon of oil over. Season with salt and pepper and distribute the oil evenly with your hands.

3 Put the potatoes in the oven for 40 minutes.

4 Heat the rest of the oil in a large pan or wok. Add the onions and garlic and fry for 1 minute. Add the celery and sweet potatoes and fry for 1 minute.

5 Add the pork mince and fry until the meat is no longer pink. Stir in the flour and cook for 1 minute.

6 Add the cider, stock, thyme and water. Season well with salt and pepper. Bring to the boil and the sauce should thicken. Turn down to simmer, for 10 minutes, with a lid on the pan.

7 Pour the pork mixture into the casserole dish. Unroll the pastry and place over the top of the pork. Brush the top with beaten egg and pierce a hole in the centre to let out the steam.

8 Place in the oven for 25 minutes, until the pastry is cooked and browned on top. Serve with the potatoes and green veg.

BEN & NICOLE: "I thought pie with pastry was supposed to be difficult. Great idea to use ready-made puff pastry, really tasty too. We all cleared our plates."

£ 1.33 /PERSON | SERVES 4 | EASE ★★★★★ | PREP 40 MINS | COOK 35 MINS

HONEY SESAME CHICKEN WITH CARROT SALAD

These chicken thighs could also go really well with the 'Sweet Potato Rice', see p116, or the 'Potato salad', see p32.

WHERE ON EARTH: Sesame seeds are kept near the baking section of the supermarket.

4 medium **potatoes** cut into chunks

2 tablespoons **olive oil**

8 medium-sized **chicken thighs (skin on)**

2 tablespoons **honey**

1 tablespoon **sesame seeds**

BBQ SAUCE

1 tablespoon **olive oil**

1 **onion**, chopped

1 clove **garlic**, finely chopped

400g tin **chopped tomatoes**

1 tablespoon **Worcestershire sauce**

1 tablespoon **tomato purée**

1 teaspoon **paprika**

1 teaspoon **granulated sugar**

CARROT AND APPLE SALAD

3 medium **carrots**, grated

3 **red apples**, cored and grated

5 **spring onions**, chopped

2 tablespoons freshly chopped **basil**

juice of ½ **lemon**

1 tablespoon **olive oil**

1 Preheat the oven to 200°C fan/220°C/ gas 7.

2 Put the potatoes on a large baking tray, drizzle with a tablespoon of oil and season well. Distribute the oil around with your hands. Put in the oven for 35 minutes.

3 Put the other tablespoon of oil in a large frying pan and fry the chicken thighs on a medium heat, skin side down, for 10 minutes. Turn them over and cover with a lid and cook on the flesh side for 10 minutes.

4 Meanwhile, make the BBQ sauce. Heat the oil in a saucepan and fry the onions and garlic until the onions begin to soften. Add the rest of the ingredients and bring to the boil. Simmer gently for 5 minutes.

5 Make the carrot salad by simply mixing the ingredients together and season well. Set aside.

6 Turn the chicken thighs over and sprinkle with the honey and sesame seeds. Turn over and fry on the skin side for 2–3 minutes until the honey is really browned. Be careful not to burn them at this stage.

7 Everything should be ready to serve together.

BEEF AND TOMATO PIE WITH POTATO CRUSH

If you make shortcrust pastry, the oven should be at 180°C fan/200°C/gas 6.

1 tablespoon **olive oil**

1 **onion**, sliced

500g **minced beef**

6 large **tomatoes**, each cut into 8

1 tablespoon **flour** (GF option)

1 mug (300ml) **water**

1 clove **garlic**, finely chopped

1 teaspoon **granulated sugar**

1 sprig **fresh rosemary**

1 **beef stock cube** (GF option)

1 pack **puff pastry** or **home-made short-crust**, see p37 (GF option)

1 beaten **egg**

4 large **potatoes**, cut into chunks

25g **butter** (measure using packet)

1 mug (75g) grated **Cheddar cheese**

green beans to serve

1 Preheat the oven to 200°C fan/220°C/gas 7.

2 Heat the oil in a large pan, or wok, and fry the onions until they begin to brown.

3 Add the beef and fry until quite browned.

4 Add the tomatoes to the pan and cook for 1 minute. Season well.

5 Add the flour and stir well. Add the water, garlic, sugar, rosemary and stock and bring to the boil. Place in a casserole dish.

6 Unroll the pastry and place over the meat. Brush the top with beaten egg.

7 Place in the oven for 20–25 minutes until the pastry is nicely browned.

8 Meanwhile, put the potatoes in a pan of boiling, salted water, bring to the boil and then turn down to simmer for 10 minutes. Drain and return to the pan.

9 Cook the green beans.

10 Lightly mash the potatoes. Add the butter and cheese, season well and stir gently. Serve with the pie.

CREAMY PORK AND MUSHROOM STEW

Not peeling potatoes saves time and energy. There are many nutrients in the skin of the potato, so you can comfort yourself that, by leaving the skin intact, you are giving your family some extra goodness.

1 tablespoon **olive oil**

4 rashers **unsmoked streaky bacon**, chopped

1 **onion**, sliced

750g **pork shoulder**, cut into cubes, or **stewing pork**

1 tablespoon **flour** (GF option)

1½ mugs (450ml) **water**

300ml **double cream**

8 **mushrooms**, sliced

1 clove **garlic**, chopped

1 **vegetable stock cube** (GF option)

1 tablespoon freshly chopped **parsley** or 1 teaspoon **dried parsley**

2 sprigs **fresh thyme** or ½ teaspoon **dried thyme**

5 medium **potatoes**, cut into chunks

50g **butter** (measure using packet)

6 **carrots**, sliced

1 head **broccoli**

1 Preheat the oven to 180°C fan/200°C/gas 6.

2 Heat the oil in a hob-to-oven casserole and fry the bacon and onions until they begin to brown.

3 Add the meat and cook until no longer pink on the outsides. Add the flour and mix well.

4 Add the water, cream, mushrooms, garlic, stock, parsley and thyme. Season well with salt and pepper. Bring to the boil. Place in the oven, with a lid on, for 1½ hours.

5 When the casserole is almost done, put the potatoes in boiling, salted water, bring to the boil and then turn down to simmer for 10 minutes.

6 Drain the potatoes and return to the pan. Crush them with a potato masher, so that lots of them stay almost whole. Add the butter, allow it to melt and gently stir in.

7 Put the carrots and broccoli on to cook.

CHICKEN CHAPATIS

Add a little more chilli powder, if you like your food spicy.

WHERE ON EARTH: Chapatis are usually in the 'bread section' next to tortilla wraps and pitta bread.

MARINADE

1 clove **garlic**, finely chopped

1 teaspoon **cumin**

1 teaspoon **turmeric**

1 teaspoon **coriander**

1/2 teaspoon **chilli powder**

1 tablespoon freshly grated **ginger**

2 tablespoons **olive oil**

3 **chicken breasts**, cut into strips

TOMATO CHUTNEY

1 tablespoon **olive oil**

1 **onion**, sliced

1 **apple**, unpeeled and chopped into small chunks

2 **tomatoes**, chopped

1 tablespoon **white wine vinegar**

1 tablespoon **granulated sugar**

RAITA

300ml **Greek yogurt**

1 tablespoon freshly chopped **mint**

1/4 **cucumber**, chopped into small chunks

6 **chapatis**

1 **Little Gem lettuce**, cut into strips

2 **spring onions**, chopped

1 Mix the garlic, cumin, tumeric, coriander, chilli powder, ginger and one tablespoon of oil in a bowl. Add the chicken pieces and mix. Leave to stand.

2 Meanwhile, make the chutney. Heat the oil in a small saucepan, add the onions and fry until they begin to brown. Add the apples and tomatoes and cook gently for 4–5 minutes. Add the vinegar and sugar and cook for a further 2 minutes. Set to one side until needed.

3 Mix together the raita ingredients.

4 Heat the other tablespoon of oil in a large frying pan and add the chicken pieces. Cook for 2–3 minutes.

5 Serve on the chapatis with the salad, raita and chutney.

STEVE & CANDY: "Loved these. I used the leftover chutney on a cheese sandwich."

LAMB MEATBALLS WITH SWEET POTATO RICE

If you want this to go a bit further, add 1 slice of wholemeal bread, made into breadcrumbs, to the meatball mix.

ONE MORE THING: You can prepare the meatballs and tomato sauce beforehand (during baby's nap time) and store in the fridge.

1 large **sweet potato**, peeled and cut into small chunks

1 tablespoon **olive oil**

TOMATO SAUCE

1 tablespoon **olive oil**

1 **onion**, sliced

1/2 **fat red chilli**, deseeded and finely chopped (optional)

1 clove **garlic**, chopped

6 **tomatoes**, chopped

1 dessertspoon **tomato purée**

1 teaspoon **granulated sugar**

salt and **pepper**

MEATBALLS

500g **lamb mince**

1 tablespoon **curry paste** (mild or hot, depending on taste) (GF option)

1 **egg yolk**

1/2 **onion**, grated

1 tablespoon **olive oil**

11/2 mugs (375g) **basmati rice**

1 teaspoon **pilau rice seasoning** (optional)

1 Preheat the oven to 200°C fan/220°C/gas 7.

2 Put the sweet potatoes on a baking tray and sprinkle with the oil and season well. Mix with your hands to distribute the oil and seasoning. Place in the oven for 25–30 minutes until browned.

3 To make the sauce, heat the oil in a saucepan and fry the onions until they begin to soften. Add the rest of the ingredients and bring to the boil. Simmer for 5 minutes. Blitz with a hand-held blender. Set aside until needed.

4 Mix together the meatball ingredients. Form into 20 balls.

5 Put the rice on to cook, see p20.

6 Heat the oil in a frying pan and fry the meatballs until they are browned all over.

7 Once the rice is cooked, mix in the roasted sweet potatoes.

8 Serve the rice with the meatballs and the tomato sauce.

OLD CLASSICS

We all want the comfort of cooking the familiar and well-loved old classics: Stew and Dumplings, Shepherds Pie, Toad in the Hole, etc. Maybe they remind us of our childhood when we did not have to do all the work! There are also step-by-step timings for Roast Chicken dinner which will, hopefully, be of help.

£1.41 /PERSON | SERVES 4 | EASE ★★★★★ | PREP 30 MINS | COOK 3½ HRS | OK TO FREEZE | GF OPTION

SLOW-COOK ROAST PORK

When choosing pork for this recipe, don't avoid the pieces of meat with fat in them. The fat contains lots of flavour and you can skim off the excess from the surface of the liquid before making the gravy.

ONE MORE THING: To make crackling, once the pork is cooked, take the skin off and place it on a greased baking tray. Put in the oven with the potatoes and it will be good and crisp.

1kg **whole pork shoulder**

1 **apple**, cored and cut into 8

1 **onion**, cut into 8

2 mugs (600ml) **water**

1 teaspoon **fennel seeds**

4 large **potatoes**, peeled and cut into chunks

6 **carrots**, peeled and cut into chunks

2 tablespoons **olive oil**

25g softened **butter** (measure using packet)

1 tablespoon **flour** (GF option)

1 head **broccoli**

1 Preheat the oven to 180°C fan/200°C/gas 6.

2 Put the pork, apple, onion, water and fennel seeds into a large casserole dish. Season with salt and pepper. Place the lid on the casserole and put in the oven for 30 minutes. After 30 minutes, turn the heat down to 150°C fan/170°C/gas 3 and cook for a further 3½ hours.

3 30 minutes before the end of the cooking time, put the potatoes and carrots in a pan of boiling, salted water. Bring to the boil and simmer for 10 minutes. Drain the potatoes, but retain the cooking water for the gravy.

4 Put a roasting tin in the oven, with the oil in, to heat up.

5 Take the meat out of the oven and turn the oven up to 200°C fan/220°C/gas 7.

6 Gently add the potatoes and carrots into the preheated tray. Carefully turn over the veg to coat with the oil. Return to the oven for 25–30 minutes, until the veg is browned.

7 Pour the liquid out of the casserole dish into a saucepan. Leave the meat in the casserole to keep warm. In a bowl, mix the butter and the flour together to make a paste. Add to the saucepan and stir well. Bring to the boil; the gravy should thicken. Add some of the potato water if necessary. Taste and, if needed, add some vegetable stock (cube or concentrated liquid). Set to one side until needed.

8 Put the broccoli in a pan of boiling, salted water and simmer for 5 minutes.

PETER & BERNICE: "This is now a family favourite — very popular. Good to have something you can safely leave in the oven and go out for a while, come back and it's cooked."

120

ONE-POT BEEF COBBLER

This is a really homely dish. Great for winter evenings to warm your cockles!

WHERE ON EARTH: Suet can be found with the flour in the 'baking section' of the supermarket.

1 tablespoon **olive oil**

2 **onions**, sliced

500g **minced beef**

4 medium **carrots**, chopped

1 tablespoon **flour**

1 mug (150g) defrosted **frozen peas**

6 **mushrooms**, sliced

2 mugs (600ml) **water**

1 **beef stock cube**

1 teaspoon **dried mixed herbs**

salt and **pepper**

1½ mugs (300g) **self-raising flour**

¾ mug (115g) **suet**

pinch **salt**

1 teaspoon **dried basil** or **coriander**

¾ mug (225ml) **water**

1 beaten **egg**

1 Preheat the oven to 180°C fan/200°C/gas 6.

2 Heat the oil in a hob-to-oven casserole. Fry the onion in the oil until soft.

3 Add the mince and carrots and cook until the meat is no longer pink. Add the flour and stir well.

4 Add the peas, mushrooms, water, stock, herbs, salt and pepper. Stir well and simmer for 10 minutes.

5 To make the dumpling top, put the flour, suet, salt and herbs in a dish and stir well. Add water a little at a time and mix. Add just enough water to make a soft dough.

6 Turn out the mixture onto a floured surface and form a ball. Cut into eight and form into balls.

7 Gently place them on the top of the meat mixture and brush the top with beaten egg.

8 Bake in the oven for 25–30 minutes, or until the crust is browned.

JOE & SARAH: "This was my first time making dumplings. They were surprisingly easy and so very tasty that you would have thought I had spent a lot of time making this dish."

BEEF AND MUSHROOM CASSEROLE

1 tablespoon **olive oil**

1 **onion**, sliced

1 clove **garlic**, finely chopped

4 rashers **streaky bacon**, cut into chunks

750g **stewing steak**, cubed

1 tablespoon **flour** (GF option)

½ x 250g pack **mushrooms**, sliced

2 mugs (600ml) **water**

2 **beef stock cubes** (GF option)

1 tablespoon **tomato purée**

2 sprigs **fresh rosemary**

4 large **potatoes**

1 Preheat the oven to 160°C fan/180°C/gas 4.

2 Heat the oil in a large pan, or hob-to-oven casserole. Add the onions, garlic and bacon and fry until the onions begin to soften.

3 Add the beef and cook until no longer pink on the outside. Add the flour and stir well.

4 Add the mushrooms, beef stock, tomato purée and rosemary. Season well with salt and pepper. If you have used a saucepan, tip the contents into a casserole dish.

5 Put a lid on the casserole and place in the oven for 1½ hours. Check half way through and stir. Add a little more water if necessary.

6 Put the potatoes in the oven to cook for the last hour of the cooking time.

£ 1.56 /PERSON | SERVES 6 | EASE ★★☆☆☆ | PREP 30 MINS | COOK 90 MINS | OK TO FREEZE | GF OPTION

SIMPLE BEEF CURRY

1 tablespoon **olive oil**

2 large **onions**, sliced

1kg **stewing beef**, cubed

2 tablespoons **rogan josh curry paste** (use Madras if you like it hot) (GF option)

1 **beef stock cube** (GF option) + 1 mug (300ml) **boiling water**

400g tin **chopped tomatoes**

basmati rice, see p20

yogurt and **naan breads** (GF option)

1. Preheat the oven to 180°C fan/200°C/gas 6.

2. Heat the oil in a large hob-to-oven casserole dish. Fry the onions until they begin to soften.

3. Add the beef and cook until it is no longer pink on the outside. Add the curry paste and cook for 30 seconds.

4. Add the water, stock and tomatoes. Bring to the boil. Put a lid on the pan and place in the oven for 1½ hours.

5. Serve with the rice, yogurt and naan bread.

TOAD IN THE HOLE WITH COX'S APPLES

The secret of good 'Toad In the Hole' is a hot oven and hot fat!

ONE MORE THING: You could serve with some green vegetables instead of the baked beans. Alternatively, if you want to make gravy from scratch, go to the video link below.

BATTER

1 mug (200g) **self-raising flour**

4 large **eggs**

pinch of **salt**

¼ mug (75ml) **milk** + ½ mug (150ml) **water**

2 tablespoons **Trex**

12 thick **pork sausages**, each cut in half

3 Cox's **apples**, cut into wedges

400g tin **baked beans**

1 Preheat the oven to 230°C fan/250°C/gas 9.

2 Beat together the batter ingredients until smooth. The mixture should look as thin as single cream.

3 Put the Trex in a large roasting tin. Place in the oven for 10 minutes. Put the sausages and apples in the hot fat. Return to the oven for 10 minutes.

4 Take the roasting tin out of the oven and pour the batter in. It should bubble around the edges as you pour it in.

5 Put back into the oven and cook for 20–25 minutes, or until browned. The mixture should rise around the edges.

6 Serve with the beans.

PETER & BERNICE: "This is the first time I have made a Yorkshire pudding that has risen. Yippee!"

WATCH A VIDEO ON HOW TO MAKE GRAVY
NOSHBOOKS.COM/GRAVY

STEW AND SUET DUMPLINGS

This uses just one pot and includes all the veg you need for the meal.

ONE MORE THING: The stew is fine to freeze, but not the dumplings.

WHERE ON EARTH: Suet is in the 'baking section' at the supermarket.

STEW

1 tablespoon **olive oil**

2 **onions**, sliced

500g **stewing beef**, cubed

1 tablespoon **flour**

3 mugs (900ml) **water**

2 **beef stock cubes**

3 **carrots**, sliced

2 **potatoes**, cut into chunks

1 **courgette**, sliced

3 sticks **celery**, sliced

1 teaspoon **dried mixed herbs**

1 mug (150g) defrosted **frozen peas**

DUMPLINGS

1 mug (200g) **self-raising flour**

1/4 teaspoon **salt**

1/2 mug (75g) **suet**

1/4 mug (75ml) **water**

2 tablespoons freshly chopped **parsley**

1 Heat the oil in a large saucepan. Add the onions and fry until they begin to soften.

2 Add the meat and cook until it is no longer pink on the outside. Add the flour and mix.

3 Add the rest of the stew ingredients, apart from the peas, season, and bring to the boil. Simmer gently, with a lid on the pan, for 1½ hours. Stir occasionally and check that the liquid has not boiled away and nothing is sticking.

4 Make the dumplings by mixing together the flour, salt and suet in a bowl. Add the water a little at a time, just enough to make a soft dough. Form into 8 balls.

5 15 minutes before the end of the cooking time, stir in the peas and then place the dumplings onto the stew. Replace the lid and cook for the rest of the time.

6 Sprinkle over the chopped parsley.

BEN & NICOLE: "I thought this would be really complicated, but it is so simple. The kids loved it, Toby especially likes the dumplings. One in each hand!"

**WATCH A VIDEO OF MAKING DUMPLINGS AT
NOSHBOOKS.COM/DUMPLINGS**

CHICKEN AND LEEK PIE

SHORTCRUST PASTRY

1³/₄ mugs (340g) **self-raising flour**

175g **cold butter** (measure using packet)

1 beaten **egg** +
¹/₄ mug (75ml) **water**

¹/₄ teaspoon **salt**

4 medium **potatoes**, cut into chunks

3 tablespoons **olive oil**

1 **onion**, chopped

2 **leeks**, sliced

3 **chicken breasts**, cut into bite-sized pieces

6 **mushrooms**, sliced

1 dessertspoon **flour**

300ml **double cream**

¹/₂ mug (150ml) **water** +
1 **chicken stock cube**

1 tablespoon freshly chopped **parsley** or **basil**

1 beaten **egg**, to brush the top

green beans

1   Make the pastry, see p37.

2   Heat the oven to 180°C fan/200°C/gas 6.

3   Put the potatoes on a large baking tray, sprinkle with 1 tablespoon of oil, season with salt and pepper, mix together and then spread out. Place in the oven for 45 minutes.

4   Heat the rest of the oil in a large saucepan or wok. Fry the onions and leeks until they begin to soften.

5   Add the chicken and the mushrooms and cook until the chicken is no longer pink.

6   Add the flour and mix well. Add the cream, water and stock. Bring to the boil, the sauce should thicken. Take off the heat, season well and add the herbs. Transfer to a large casserole dish.

7   Roll out the pastry and place on top of the casserole. Make a small hole in the centre to allow the steam to escape. Pinch the edges and brush with the beaten egg.

8   Place in the oven for 25–30 minutes, the pastry should be slightly browned.

9   5 minutes before the end of the cooking time, put the beans on to cook.

BEN & NICOLE: "I have never made pie before. I have always wanted to. This was my first time to make pastry too. Not as difficult as I thought, in fact, quite easy. The pie tasted awesome. Bella is a great fan and has requested that we have this every week."

WATCH A VIDEO OF MAKING PASTRY AT NOSHBOOKS.COM/PASTRY

BEN'S DESPERATE DAN COW PIE

Ever read the Dandy, with Desperate Dan? He famously chowed down on Cow Pie. Although this recipe doesn't have the same caricatured 'pastry horns' I think it comes pretty close to what Dan would have eaten! This has been Ben's favourite meal for years. He requests it every year for his birthday.

ONE MORE THING: I would never recommend making puff pastry from scratch, as it takes so long, but making shortcrust is very easy. Give it a go.

---

2 tablespoons **olive oil**

1 **onion**, sliced

750g **stewing beef**

2 mugs (600ml) **water**

1 **beef stock cube**

5 **carrots**, sliced

6 medium **potatoes**, thinly sliced

25g softened **butter** (measure using packet)

1 tablespoon **flour**

SHORTCRUST PASTRY

175g **butter** (measure using packet)

1 ¾ mugs (340g) **self-raising flour**

1 beaten **egg** + ¼ mug (75ml) **water**

1 Heat the oil in a large saucepan and fry the onions until they become soft and a little brown.

2 Add the meat and fry until no longer pink on the outside.

3 Add the 2 mugs of water, stock and carrots and bring to the boil. Put a lid on the pan and turn down to simmer for 1½ hours.

4 Add the potatoes to some boiling, salted water and bring to the boil. Turn down to simmer for 8–10 minutes until the potatoes are tender. Drain and return to the pan.

5 Heat the oven to 180°C fan/200°C/gas 6.

6 Mix the softened butter and flour together, add to the meat and stir well. The gravy should thicken. If most of the liquid has boiled away, add another mug of water.

7 Pour the meat mixture into the bottom of a large casserole dish. Put the cooked potatoes on top.

8 Make the pastry, see p37. Roll out the pastry and place over the potatoes. Cut to size and pinch the edges of the pastry. Make a little hole in the centre for the steam to get out. This stops the pastry from going soggy. Brush the top with beaten egg.

9 Place in the oven for 25 minutes, or until the pastry is browned on top.

WATCH A VIDEO OF MAKING PASTRY AT
NOSHBOOKS.COM/PASTRY

£0.83 /PERSON • SERVES 4 • EASE ★★☆☆☆ • PREP 25 MINS • OK TO FREEZE

SPAGHETTI BOLOGNESE

1 tablespoon **olive oil**

1 **onion**, chopped

2 cloves **garlic**, chopped

500g **minced beef**

400g tin **chopped tomatoes**

2 tablespoons **tomato purée**

6 **mushrooms**, sliced

1 teaspoon **dried mixed herbs**

1 teaspoon **granulated sugar**

1 **beef stock cube**

1 tablespoon **Worcestershire sauce**

250g **spaghetti**

1 Heat the oil in a large saucepan and fry the onion and garlic for 1 minute.

2 Add the mince and cook until the meat is no longer pink.

3 Add the tomatoes, tomato purée, mushrooms, herbs and sugar. Crumble the stock cube into the pan, add the Worcestershire sauce and stir well. Bring to boil, then simmer gently for 10 minutes. Season well with salt and pepper.

4 Put the spaghetti on to cook, see p21.

5 Drain the pasta and add a little olive oil to stop it sticking together. Serve on a plate with the Bolognese sauce on the top. You can grate Parmesan, or Cheddar cheese, over the top if you like.

£1.53 /PERSON | SERVES 4 | EASE ★★☆☆☆ | PREP 25 MINS | COOK 25 MINS | OK TO FREEZE ❄

EASY SHEPHERD'S PIE

2 large **sweet potatoes**, cut into chunks

2 large **white potatoes**, cut into chunks

25g **butter** (measure using packet)

1 tablespoon **olive oil**

1 large **onion**, chopped

500g **lamb mince**

1 tablespoon **flour**

1 mug (300ml) **water**

1 **lamb** or **vegetable stock cube**

2 tablespoons **Worcestershire sauce**

3–4 sprigs **fresh thyme** or ½ teaspoon **dried thyme**

1 Preheat the oven to 180°C fan/200°C/gas 6. Grease a casserole dish.

2 Put the potatoes in boiling, salted water, add salt and simmer for 10 minutes. Drain and return to the pan. Add the butter and squash gently with a potato masher, no need to mash. Stir to distribute the butter. Leave to one side until needed.

3 Heat the oil in a large pan or wok. Add the onion and fry until it begins to brown. Add the mince and fry until it is no longer pink.

4 Add the flour and stir well to distribute. Cook for 30 seconds. Add the water, stock cube, Worcestershire sauce, thyme and season well. Bring to the boil and the sauce should thicken.

5 Pour into the bottom of the casserole dish. Put the potatoes on top and spread them out.

6 Place in the oven for 20–25 minutes until brown.

7 Serve with green vegetables.

BANGERS AND SWEET POTATO MASH

2 large **sweet potatoes**, peeled and cut into chunks

2 large **potatoes**, cut into chunks

25g **butter** (measure using packet)

1 tablespoon **olive oil**

8–10 large **pork sausages**

1 **onion**, chopped

400g tin **baked beans**

2 tablespoons **Worcestershire sauce**

1 dessertspoon **golden syrup**

¼ mug (75ml) **water**

1   Put the potatoes in boiling, salted water, bring to the boil and turn down to simmer for 10 minutes. Drain and return to the pan.

2   Add the butter and gently squash the potatoes with a masher, but no need to completely mash. Stir in the butter and distribute well. Season with salt and pepper. Leave in the pan with a lid on, until needed.

3   Heat the oil in a large pan or wok. Fry the sausages until they are browned. Add the onions and fry. Stir frequently. Once the onions begin to soften, add the beans, Worcestershire sauce, syrup, water and salt and pepper. Simmer for 2–3 minutes.

4   Serve with the crushed potato.

HEALTHY FISH AND CHIPS

4 large **potatoes**, cut into wedges

1 tablespoon **olive oil**

4 **cod steaks**

3 slices **wholemeal bread**, made into breadcrumbs (GF option)

30g melted **butter** (measure using packet)

zest of a **lemon**

1 tablespoon **sesame seeds**

1 **egg**, beaten

2 mugs (300g) defrosted **frozen peas**

1   Preheat the oven to 180°C fan/200°C/ gas 6.

2   Place the potatoes on a baking tray. Sprinkle with oil, salt and pepper. Mix everything together and stand the wedges on their skins, this helps them not to stick to the tray. Place in the oven for 35 minutes.

3   Meanwhile, mix together the bread-crumbs, melted butter, lemon zest, and sesame seeds. Season with salt and pepper.

4   Put the beaten eggs onto a plate and coat each piece of fish with the egg. Dip them into the breadcrumb mix. Place on another baking tray and place in the oven for 20 minutes. The breadcrumbs should be nicely browned. If you are using thicker fish steaks, you will need to leave them in the oven for 25 minutes.

LASAGNE WITH ADDED SMOKY BACON

4 rashers **smoked bacon**, chopped

1 **onion**, chopped

1 **carrot**, finely chopped

2 cloves **garlic**, chopped

2 tablespoons **olive oil**

500g **minced beef**

400g tin **chopped tomatoes**

1 tablespoon **tomato purée**

1 **beef stock cube** (GF option)

¼ teaspoon **paprika**

50g **butter** (measure using packet)

2 heaped tablespoons **flour** (GF option)

2 mugs (600ml) **milk**

2 **mozzarella** balls, torn up

9–12 **lasagne sheets** (GF option)

1 If you have a food processor, put the bacon, onion, carrot and garlic in the processor and blitz for 30 seconds. There is no need to chop.

2 Heat the oil in a wok, or large saucepan, and fry the onion, bacon, carrot and garlic until they begin to brown.

3 Add the mince and cook until the meat is no longer pink.

4 Add the tomatoes, tomato purée, stock and paprika. Season well and simmer gently for 10 minutes.

5 Preheat the oven to 180°C fan/200°C/gas 6.

6 To make the white sauce, put the butter and flour in a saucepan and gently heat until it forms a paste. Take off the heat and add the milk. Stir with a whisk and return to the heat. Gently bring to the boil, stirring all the time. The sauce will thicken. Season well with salt and pepper.

7 Put half the meat mix in the bottom of a casserole dish and place a layer of lasagne sheets over the top. Pour half the sauce on top, then place another layer of lasagne sheets. Repeat the whole process again. Place the torn mozzarella on the top and season well.

8 Place in the oven for 20–25 minutes until the cheese is browned.

ANDY & HEATHER: "Lasagne with a bit of a twist, the children really like the bacon in it."

£1.93 /PERSON SERVES 6 EASE ★★★★☆ PREP 45 MINS COOK 120 MINS OK TO FREEZE ❄

ROAST CHICKEN DINNER

3kg **whole chicken**

1 mug (300ml) **boiling water**

1 tablespoon **olive oil**

1 teaspoon **dried rosemary** or a sprig of **fresh rosemary**

STUFFING

1 mug (300ml) **boiling water**

1 **onion**, cut into wedges

3 slices **wholemeal bread**, made into breadcrumbs

1 teaspoon **mixed dried herbs**

400g **sausage meat**

8 **mushrooms**, sliced

salt and **pepper**

6 large **potatoes**, cut into chunks

6–8 **carrots**, chopped

1 head **broccoli**, cut into florets

25g **butter**, softened (measure using packet)

1 tablespoon **flour**

1 Preheat the oven to 180°C fan/200°C/gas 6.

2 Put the chicken in a roasting dish and add the water. Brush the top with oil and sprinkle over with some rosemary. Season with salt and pepper. Put in the oven with a lid or foil. Cook for 1 hour. Take off the lid and cook for a further hour.

3 To make the stuffing, put the water and onions in a pan and simmer for 5 minutes. Add the rest of the stuffing ingredients to the pan and mix together. Place in a greased casserole dish. Put in the oven for 75 minutes, or until browned. Stir once during the cooking time.

4 Put the potatoes on a tray and sprinkle with oil and season. Mix together to make sure all the surfaces of the potatoes are covered. Place in the oven for 1 hour.

5 Put the carrots and broccoli on to cook. Once cooked, drain, but retain the cooking liquid and return to the pans to keep warm.

6 Take the chicken out after 2 hours and transfer onto a large plate. Cover with foil to keep it warm.

7 In a bowl, mix together the butter and flour to make a paste. Mix some of the carrot water and the juices from the bottom of the roasting tin in a saucepan. Bring to the boil and add the butter and flour mixture. Whisk together and the gravy should thicken.

TIMELINE

10:45am	11:30am	12:15pm	12:30pm	1:10pm	1:15pm	1:15pm
Chicken in oven	stuffing in oven	stir stuffing, return to oven	potatoes in oven	carrots on (drain once cooked and return to the pan)	chicken out and make gravy	broccoli on to cook

STEAK AND ALE CASSEROLE

If you want to slow cook this while you go out, you can put in the oven for 40 minutes on 180°C fan/200°C/gas 6, then turn the oven to 150°C fan/170°C/gas 3 and cook for a further 3–4 hours.

2 tablespoons **olive oil**

2 **onions**, sliced

1kg **stewing steak**

3 tablespoons **flour** (GF option)

400ml bottle **fruity ale** (GF option)

2 mugs (600ml) **water**

2 **beef stock cubes** (GF option)

3 sticks **celery**, roughly chopped

4 large **carrots**, cut into chunks

2 large **parsnips**, cut into chunks

4 sprigs **thyme**

7 large **potatoes**, cut into chunks

50g **butter** (measure using packet)

1 head **broccoli**, cut into florets

1 ½ mugs (250g) defrosted **frozen peas**

1 Preheat the oven to 180°C fan/200°C/gas 6.

2 Heat the oil in a large hob-to-oven casserole dish. Fry the onions until they begin to soften.

3 Add the meat and cook until the meat is no longer pink on the outside. Stir frequently.

4 Add the flour and stir until it is evenly distributed. Add the ale and stir well.

5 Add the water, ale, stock, celery, carrots, parsnips and thyme. Bring to the boil and season well.

6 Place in the preheated oven for 1½ hours.

7 When the casserole has 30 minutes left to cook, put the potatoes on to boil for 10 minutes. Drain and return to the pan. Add the butter and squash with a potato masher, but don't mash them too much.

8 Put the broccoli and peas on to cook together in another saucepan. Once cooked, drain and mix into the potato squash.

SPECIAL DAYS

Having friends around, or just fancy something a little bit fancy? This is the time to 'push the boat out' and find something a bit different. Some may take a bit more effort, others are still very simple to make. All are scrumptious.

POACHED SALMON WITH MUSTARD SAUCE AND CUCUMBER PICKLE

Lovely meal when you get the chance to eat together, without the kids.

MUSTARD SAUCE

3 tablespoons **crème fraîche**

1 teaspoon **Dijon mustard** or **wholegrain mustard**

1 tablespoon freshly chopped **basil**

2 tablespoons **white wine vinegar**

2 tablespoons **olive oil**

1 teaspoon **granulated sugar**

3 **spring onions**, chopped

10cm piece **cucumber**

2 **salmon fillets**

200g **green beans**

500g **new potatoes**

1 Mix the mustard sauce ingredients together in a bowl and set aside until needed.

2 Mix together the wine vinegar, olive oil, sugar and salt and pepper in another bowl. Add the spring onions. Cut the cucumber in half lengthways and scoop out the seed part. Cut into small chunks and add to the bowl.

3 Put the potatoes in a pan of boiling, salted water and simmer for 5 minutes. Add the beans and simmer for a further 5 minutes.

4 Put ½ mug of boiling water in a saucepan, add the salmon, season with salt and pepper, cover with a lid, and simmer for 5 minutes. Gently open up the fish with a fork to check that they are cooked in the middle.

5 Drain the veggies and serve together, as photo.

ALAN & JO: "This is brill, loved the cucumber pickle which was a real surprise. Have made it loads of times."

£ 1.65 /PERSON | SERVES 4 | EASE ★★☆☆☆ | PREP 20 MINS | COOK 60 MINS | OK TO FREEZE ❄ | GF OPTION

THAI COCONUT CHICKEN

Really quick one-pot dish. Just put everything in together, no need to cook anything on the hob, just straight in the oven.

ONE MORE THING: This makes quite a thin sauce, but is delicious.

WHERE ON EARTH: Red Thai curry paste is usually in the 'speciality foods section' at the supermarket.

---

3 **sweet potatoes**, peeled and cut into chunks

1 **onion**, cut into wedges

8 **chicken thighs (skin on)**

400ml tin **coconut milk**

1 clove **garlic**, chopped

1 tablespoon freshly grated **ginger**

juice of a **lime**

1 **chicken stock cube** (GF option)

1 tablespoon **red Thai curry paste** (GF option)

rice and **green veg** to serve

1 Preheat the oven to 180°C fan/200°C/gas 6.

2 Put the sweet potatoes and onions on the bottom of a large casserole dish. Place the chicken thighs on the top.

3 Mix the coconut milk, garlic, ginger, lime juice, stock and curry paste together. Pour over the top of the thighs.

4 Place in the oven, uncovered, for 1 hour. If the chicken thighs begin to brown too much, cover with a piece of foil.

5 Serve with rice, see p20, and green veg.

JOE & SARAH: "I love cooking Thai and the Crispy Thai chicken was certainly different from the way I would have normally cooked it, but equally, if not better, tasting. I'll certainly be using this recipe again soon."

WATCH A VIDEO OF HOW TO COOK RICE AT
NOSHBOOKS.COM/RICE

LEMON GINGER CHICKEN

juice and zest of a **lemon**

1 tablespoon **honey**

2 cloves **garlic**, finely chopped

1 tablespoon freshly grated **ginger**

1 tablespoon **olive oil**

3 **chicken breasts**

3 mugs (900ml) **water**

2 teaspoons **pilau rice seasoning** (optional)

1½ mugs (375g) **basmati rice**

200g pack **mangetout**, sliced

1 Preheat the oven to 180°C fan 200°C/gas 6. Lightly grease an ovenproof dish.

2 Mix together the lemon zest, juice, honey, garlic, ginger and oil. Place the chicken in the dish and pour the sauce over. Place in the oven for 25 minutes.

3 Meanwhile, put the water in a saucepan and bring to the boil. Add the pilau rice seasoning and the rice. Stir and bring back to the boil. Turn down to simmer, with the lid on, for 10 minutes, or until the rice is tender and all the liquid absorbed.

4 Once the rice is cooked, add the mangetout to the rice pan. Put the lid back on and leave to stand off the heat. Stir in the mangetout when you are ready to serve.

5 Once the chicken is cooked, remove from the oven and slice. Spoon over the juices and serve.

GRUYÈRE AND HERB SALMON

4 medium **potatoes**, cut into chunks

1 tablespoon **olive oil**

4 **salmon** pieces

1 tablespoon freshly chopped **parsley**

1 tablespoon freshly chopped **basil**

½ mug (40g) grated **Gruyère cheese**

green beans

1 Preheat the oven to 180°C fan/200°C/gas 6.

2 Put the potatoes on a baking tray and sprinkle with the oil. Distribute well and season with salt and pepper. Place in the oven for 35–40 minutes.

3 After the potatoes have been in the oven for 25 minutes, heat a little oil in a frying pan. Add the salmon steaks, skin side down, and fry for 3 minutes on a medium heat.

4 Mix the parsley, basil and cheese. Sprinkle on the top of the steaks. Place under a hot grill for 5–6 minutes. Check to see that the salmon is cooked through; this, of course, depends on the thickness.

5 Serve with the potatoes and cooked green beans.

£ 1.70 /PERSON — SERVES 4 — EASE ★★★★★ — PREP 35 MINS — OK TO FREEZE ❄ — GF OPTION

MINI MEAT LOAVES

TOMATO SAUCE

1 tablespoon **olive oil**

1 **onion**, chopped

1 clove **garlic**, finely chopped

4 **tomatoes**, chopped

2 teaspoons **tomato purée**

1 teaspoon **granulated sugar**

1 teaspoon **dried mixed herbs**

1 **vegetable stock cube** (GF option)

¼ mug (75ml) **water**

MEAT LOAVES

500g **minced beef**

1 tablespoon freshly chopped **basil**

1 clove **garlic**, finely chopped

1 **egg yolk**

250g **mozzarella cheese**, chopped

200g **streaky bacon**

1 tablespoon **olive oil**

new potatoes or **baked potatoes**

green beans or **sugar snaps**

1 Make the tomato sauce. Heat the oil in a saucepan and fry the onions and garlic until they begin to soften. Add the rest of the ingredients and bring to the boil. Turn down to simmer for 10 minutes. Whizz with the blender.

2 Mix together the beef, basil, garlic and egg in a bowl and season well.

3 Stir the chopped mozzarella into the mixture.

4 Spread the bacon slices on a large piece of cling film. Put the beef mixture on top and then roll the bacon around it to make one long sausage.

5 Unfold the cling film and cut in half.

6 Put the potatoes and greens on to boil.

7 Heat the oil in a large frying pan and fry the mini meat loaves on a low heat for 15 minutes. Turn frequently to make sure the bacon does not get too browned. Slice into 8 before serving (see photo).

8 Serve with the potatoes, sugar snaps and tomato sauce.

ALAN & JO: "Mini Meat loaves, what a great idea to have individual meat loaves. Delicious. We loved the tomato sauce, it would be great with pasta too."

SPICED CHICKEN & HERB COUSCOUS

This recipe works best when you use fresh herbs. They are so easy to keep in pots in the garden, or on a window sill.

juice of ½ a **lemon**

1 teaspoon **cumin**

1 teaspoon **coriander**

½ teaspoon **paprika**

1 clove **garlic**, finely chopped

3 **chicken breasts**

1 mug (200g) **couscous**

zest of a **lemon**

1 **chicken stock cube**

2 mugs (600ml) **boiling water**

1 tablespoon **olive oil**

1 **red onion**, chopped

1 **yellow pepper**, chopped

2 **tomatoes**, chopped

200g **feta cheese**, crumbled

1 tablespoon freshly chopped **basil**

1 tablespoon freshly chopped **coriander**

1 tablespoon **olive oil**

1. Mix together, in a bowl, the lemon juice, cumin, coriander, paprika and garlic. Coat the chicken breasts and leave to stand for 5 minutes.

2. Put the couscous in a bowl with the lemon zest and stock. Add the boiling water. Put a plate over the bowl and leave to stand for 4 minutes. The water should be absorbed. If not, leave a little longer.

3. Heat the oil in a frying pan and fry the onions and peppers until they begin to brown. Take out of the pan and set to one side.

4. Add the chicken breasts to the frying pan. Cook on a high heat for 2 minutes each side and then turn the heat down to medium. Pour the rest of the marinade into the pan. Put a lid over the chicken breasts and cook each side for 4 minutes.

5. Meanwhile, add the onions, peppers, tomatoes, feta, basil, coriander and olive oil to the couscous and mix well.

6. When the chicken breasts are cooked, cut them into strips and serve on top of the couscous.

ANDY & HEATHER: "We really like this dish. Nathan even requested it for his birthday dinner."

MEZZE

12 PITTA BREADS TO DIP £0.90

When you have finished all the dips and pâtés, heat the **pitta breads** in a hot oven for 2–3 minutes. Whilst still warm, cut into strips.

VEG STICKS TO DIP £3.67

½ **cucumber**, cut into strips

3 **carrots**, cut into strips

250g pack **baby sweetcorn**

1 **pepper**, cut into strips

4 sticks **celery**, cut into strips

BEAN DIP £2.95

400g tin **cannellini beans**

1 tablespoon **Greek yogurt**

10 **anchovy fillets**

juice of ½ a **lemon**

Blitz together.

BEETROOT SALAD £1.63

250g **cooked beetroot**, cut into small chunks

½ x 200g pack **feta**, crumbled

1 tablespoon freshly chopped **basil**

1 tablespoon **olive oil**

HALLOUMI £2.17

250g pack **halloumi cheese**

1 tablespoon **olive oil**

Cut the cheese into slices, fry on a high heat, and season with salt and pepper.

PÂTÉ £1.00

200g pack **duck** or **pork pâté**

GARLIC OLIVES £0.65

30 **olives** (approx.)

1 tablespoon **olive oil**

½ clove **garlic**, finely chopped

1 tablespoon freshly chopped **basil** and **thyme**

salt and **pepper**

MACKEREL PÂTÉ £3.93

4 small **ready-cooked smoked mackerel fillets**

2 large tablespoons **crème fraîche**

pepper

juice of ½ **lemon**

1 small clove **garlic**, very finely chopped

Mash everything together, or blitz very quickly in a food processor.

HUMMUS £1.38

1 tablespoon **olive oil**

400g tin **chickpeas**

2 tablespoons **tahini paste**

1 clove **garlic**, very finely chopped

1 tablespoon **Greek yogurt**

1 teaspoon freshly chopped **basil**

juice of ½ **lemon**

1 **red pepper**, cut into chunks

Heat the oil in a frying pan and fry the peppers on a medium heat for about 5 minutes, until they are browned and soft. Using a hand-held blender or processor, blitz everything together and season well.

KIDS' PARTIES

These times are such fun! You need to be around
to enjoy them and not be in the kitchen all the time.
The parties are designed so that everything can be
made the day before. There is one party for 'littlies'
and one for young teens.

KIDS' PARTY FOOD

Children love parties and they don't need to be really hard work for us. Here are a few helpful hints. Many of them obvious, which should make the time more fun for you. Enlist the help of some other parents; they usually would rather help than stand around watching. Buy a plastic tablecloth and sit them on the floor on cushions. This means they are closer together and gives a good atmosphere. Afterwards, you just need to wipe and sweep up. Have a few clean tea-towels handy, to quickly wipe up any spills or gunge. Steer clear of the foods containing additives and you will not have a room full of hyper children.

KEEP THINGS AS SIMPLE AS POSSIBLE. Here are some food suggestions. Just choose a few, don't try to do them all at once. Buy some chipolata sausages and twist them into tiny sausages. Roast them in the oven for 25 minutes and then cut them apart. Voila, mini sausages!

VEG STICKS SEEM TO GO DOWN WELL. Cut up some carrot, celery and cucumber into sticks. Mix together a 200g pack of cream cheese and 1 dessertspoon of mango chutney. You could also add a few cherry tomatoes. Other finger food for them would be tiny cheese cubes, grapes and peeled satsumas.

SANDWICHES ARE FAIRLY STAPLE. Cream cheese, ham, tuna and mayo make good simple fillings. Cut them into shapes, if you have any cutters, otherwise, just cut off the crusts to make them more special. Eat the excess pieces to keep you going while you prepare.

CAKES AND COOKIES ARE A MUST. Make 'Butterfly Cakes' with big chocolate buttons (p228). Also, 'Crispy Oat Cookies' (p216) and 'Coffee Shop Cookies' (p220).

ROCKY ROADS. (p230) are good for older children. May be a bit much for younger ones.

BIRTHDAY CAKES. When it comes to birthday cakes, if you love making and icing cakes, being up to your elbows in fondant and food colouring, then by all means make the cake. However, don't try to be a hero! There are some fabulous cakes you can buy at the supermarket. They may be fractionally more expensive than a home made one, but will save you loads of time and energy.

I LOVE TRIFLE! Most of the helpers and parents will also love it, together with some of the kids. I've invented an almost healthy one called the 'Jelly Berry Trifle' on page 236. It's full of fruit and not too sweet – give it a try.

TO PREVENT SPILLS. In order to prevent spills, it is wise to get some individual packet drinks. Write each child's name on the box and, once they have wandered off, they can be reunited with their drink. You may see from the photos that we bought a really fun, inexpensive, pink tea set. No problem if it gets broken and I think it is going to be out on loan to a few people!

TEENS' MOVIE NIGHT

There comes a time when the children do not really want us around at their party, be it a birthday, or just a get together with their friends. We discovered, however, that they would still like us to provide the food and the means for the party! We may be allowed to be there in the background, but certainly not too visible.

MENU

CHICKEN NUGGETS AND WEDGES
(P180 & P23)

MILLIONAIRES SHORTBREAD
(P218)

ROCKY ROADS
(P230)

POPCORN (OBVIOUSLY)

GETTING KIDS INVOLVED

I started to cook when I was about 6 years old and this gave me lots of confidence when I later needed to be responsible in cooking for my family and friends. Getting kids involved with the preparation at any early age encourages their interest in cooking. I have included some fun recipes, which most kids will like. They are very simple and do-able for kids from about 3–18. One of my wonderful recipe testers, Jo, has three children and both she and her husband go out to work. As the children went through their teens, they had a family cooking-rota, so each week, everyone in the family would take a turn to cook the meal. I have to admit, I never managed to do this with my boys, but it is a great thing to aim for!

SPICED APRICOT TURKEY BURGERS

This one is really simple if you have a food processor. If you don't, it is a little more time consuming, but still worth it.

4 medium **potatoes**, cut into wedges

1 tablespoon **olive oil**

4 **burger buns** (GF option)

BURGERS

1 slice **wholemeal bread** (GF option)

1 large **onion**, quartered

2 cloves **garlic**

4 **ready-to-eat dried apricots**

450g **turkey breast**

1 teaspoon **cumin**

1 teaspoon **coriander**

1/2 **egg**, beaten

1 tablespoon **olive oil**

4 tablespoons **mayo**

1 **Little Gem lettuce**

1 Preheat the oven to 180°C fan/200°C/gas 6.

2 Put the wedges on a roasting tray. Add the oil, season, and mix everything together with your hands. Place in the oven for 30 minutes.

3 If you do not have a food processor, finely chop up the burger ingredients and mix together.

4 If you have a processor, blitz the wholemeal bread first and place in a large bowl. Next, blitz the onion, garlic and apricots together and add to the bowl.

5 Next, blitz the turkey breast; they will only need about 4–5 pulses as you don't want to make them into pulp. Mix this with the breadcrumbs and the rest of the burger ingredients and season well.

6 Form into 4–5 burger shapes. Make sure you press the mixture together well, so they don't fall apart when cooking.

7 Heat the oil in a large frying pan and add the burgers. Fry on a medium heat for 10 minutes, turning frequently.

8 Serve the burgers in the buns with the lettuce and mayo.

LUKE & RACH: "The apricots and turkey taste so great together! We often make these for the girls, but also for entertaining guests too. They're a winner with everyone. Luke would eat them every day if he could."

£0.85 /PERSON · SERVES 4 · EASE ★★☆☆☆ · PREP 25 MINS · COOK 00 MINS · GF OPTION

BEEF BURGERS WITH CRISPY FRIED ONIONS

BURGER

½ **onion**, grated

500g **minced beef**

1 **egg yolk**

3 **sun-dried tomatoes**, finely chopped

salt and **pepper**

1 teaspoon **mustard** (GF option)

1 tablespoon **olive oil**

1 tablespoon **olive oil**

25g **butter** (measure using packet)

1 large **onion**, sliced

4 **burger buns** (GF option)

1 Squeeze out any excess liquid from the onion. Mix with the rest of the ingredients for the burger. Using your hands, mix the ingredients evenly until everything sticks together. Split into 4 and form into burgers.

2 Heat a tablespoon of oil in a large frying pan. Add the burgers and cook on a medium heat for 10–12 minutes. If you have made 5 burgers, it will take less time. Turn the burgers over every 3 minutes or so, to prevent them burning.

3 Meanwhile, to make the crispy fried onions, heat the oil and butter in a small frying pan, add the onions and season well. Fry them on a medium heat until they become brown and crispy. This should take about the same length of time as the burgers will take to cook.

4 Serve together in a burger bun. Potato wedges go well, see p23. If you put these in before you begin to prepare the burgers, everything should be ready at about the same time.

CURRIED LAMB BURGERS & MANGO SALAD

BURGER

1 **onion**, grated

500g **lamb mince**

1 tablespoon **curry paste** (GF option)
(mild or hot depending on taste)

1 **egg yolk**

1 tablespoon **olive oil**

SALAD

2 **Little Gem lettuce**, sliced

4 **spring onions**, sliced

1 **mango**, peeled,
stoned and sliced

1 **fat red chilli**,
chopped

1 Squeeze the liquid from the grated onion
and mix together with all the burger
ingredients. Add just enough egg to
make everything bind together, but not
be too sloppy.

2 Form into burgers with your hands or by
using a ring.

3 Heat a tablespoon of oil in a large frying
pan and fry the burgers on a medium
heat for 8–10 minutes, depending on
how thick you have made them.

4 Serve with the salad.

CHICKEN BURGERS

1 slice **wholemeal bread** (GF option)

½ **onion**

2 **chicken breasts**

yoke of 1 **egg**

1 tablespoon freshly chopped **basil**

serve in a **bun** (GF option) with **salad** and **mayo**

1 If you have a food processor, blitz the breadcrumbs and transfer them into a bowl. Chop the onion into quarters and blitz. Squeeze out the excess liquid. Add the chicken and pulse 4–5 times. Add to the breadcrumbs, egg yoke and basil and mix together. Season well.

2 If you do not have a food processor, finely chop the breadcrumbs and chicken breasts. Grate the onion and squeeze out any excess liquid. Mix together in a bowl with the remaining burger ingredients.

3 Form into burgers. Heat a little oil in a large frying pan and cook on a medium heat for 8–10 minutes, turning occasionally. Cut into the centre of one of the burgers to check they are cooked.

 £1.14 /PERSON SERVES 4 EASE ★★☆☆☆ PREP 20 MINS COOK 25 MINS OK TO FREEZE GF OPTION

SUPER SIMPLE TUNA BAKE

2 mugs (200g) **pasta** (we used fusilli) (GF option)

1 mug (150g) defrosted **frozen peas**

2 x 160g tins **tuna**, drained

4 **spring onions**, chopped

300ml **soured cream**,

juice of ½ **lemon**

1 mug (75g) grated **Cheddar cheese**

2 small packets **ready-salted crisps**, crushed

1 Preheat the oven to 180°C fan/200°C/gas 6. Grease a large casserole dish.

2 Cook the pasta and drain, then add the peas. Put the lid on the pan and leave to one side until needed.

3 Mix together the tuna, spring onions, soured cream and lemon juice. Add to the cooked pasta and peas, season with salt and pepper, and mix gently. Pour into the greased casserole dish.

4 Spread the crisps, then the cheese, over the top of the casserole dish.

5 Place in the oven for 20–25 minutes, until the crisps and cheese are browned.

SAUSAGE AND CHESTNUT PATTIES

Use a food processor to make the patties and save time on all the chopping processes. You can freeze these when they are cold.

WHERE ON EARTH: You can buy cooked and peeled, whole chestnuts in Sainsburys. They are over the freezer counters, near the stock cubes.

3 medium **potatoes**, cut into chunks

1 medium **butternut squash**, cut into chunks

4 **tomatoes**, quartered

1 tablespoon **olive oil**

PATTIES

500g **sausage meat**

2 slices **wholemeal bread**, made into breadcrumbs

1 medium **onion**, chopped

6 **mushrooms**, chopped

1 teaspoon **mixed dried herbs**

200g pack **whole, cooked chestnuts**, roughly chopped

green veg

1 Preheat the oven to 180°C fan/200°C/gas 6.

2 Put the potatoes, butternut squash and tomatoes on a baking tray and drizzle with oil. Season with salt and pepper. Distribute the oil evenly, using your hands. Place in the oven for 50 minutes.

3 In a large bowl, mix together the pattie ingredients. Season well with salt and pepper. The mixture will be quite rustic. If you do this in a food processor, add things in the following order – onions, then mushrooms and chestnuts, then bread and finally sausage meat and herbs.

4 Form into 12 patties. Place on a greased baking tray and put in the oven for 40 minutes.

5 Serve with the roasted vegetables and cooked green veg.

ANDY & HEATHER: "These are good cold with some salad."

WATCH A VIDEO OF HOW TO PEAL A SQUASH AT
NOSHBOOKS.COM/SQUASH

WRAPS

Wraps are so quick and easy for children to make and are a good way into simple cooking. You can, of course, vary the ingredients. The recipes here just give an idea of the kinds of things to include. They work well with a bit of crunch (lettuce, cucumber, etc.), bit of sauce (hoisin, mayo, tomato sauce, BBQ or curry) and some meat. Chicken breast is easy to cook and it goes with so many different flavours.

BEN & NICOLE: "You could have so much fun doing these with kids and not get stressed at all. It's just like Bella putting her dolls in a blanket at bed-time…and then eating them. Maybe you could try using that example. Up to you!"

CAJUN CHICKEN

£0.99
/PERSON

1 tablespoon **Cajun seasoning**

2 **chicken breasts**, sliced

1 tablespoon **olive oil**

4 **spring onions**, thinly sliced

1 **red** or **yellow pepper**, thinly sliced

6 **corn tortillas**

1 **Little Gem lettuce**

4 tablespoons **soured cream**

1 Put the Cajun seasoning on a plate and dip the slices of chicken breast in. Cover evenly. Heat the oil in a frying pan and fry the chicken for 4–5 minutes, checking the thickest piece is thoroughly cooked.

2 Spread the mayo over each tortilla and divide the ingredients between them.

3 Roll up, cut each one in half, and serve.

CHICKEN & BACON

£1.23
/PERSON

1 tablespoon **olive oil**

8 rashers **streaky bacon**

2 **chicken breasts**

4 tablespoons **mayo**

8 **corn tortillas**

4 **spring onions**, sliced lengthways

1 **Cos lettuce**, pulled apart

¼ **cucumber**, cut into strips

1 Heat the oil and fry the bacon until it is crispy. Set to one side.

2 Fry the chicken breasts for 2 minutes each side on a high heat. On a low heat, cook for 4 minutes each side, with a lid on the pan. Leave to stand for a couple of minutes and then cut into thin slices.

3 Spread the mayo on the tortillas and divide the ingredients evenly between them. Roll up and serve with the wedges.

EGG & SALMON

£1.08
/PERSON

6 **corn tortilla wraps**

2 tablespoons **mayo**

1 packet **smoked salmon** (sandwich pack)

4 **hard-boiled eggs**, sliced

1 **Little Gem lettuce**

4 **spring onions**, thinly sliced

1 Spread each wrap with mayo.

2 Divide the salmon between the wraps and add the rest of the ingredients.

3 Roll each one up, cut in half, and serve.

CHICKEN QUESADILLAS AND TOMATO SALSA

1 tablespoon **olive oil**

3 **chicken breasts**, sliced

6 **mushrooms**, sliced

100g **spinach leaves**

6 small **corn tortillas** (GF option)

1 mug (75g) grated **Cheddar cheese**

guacamole (optional, depending on how old the children are and if they like spice)

SALSA

2 **tomatoes**, chopped

2 spring **onions**, chopped

1 tablespoon freshly chopped **basil**

juice of ½ **lemon**

1 dessertspoon **olive oil**

salt and **pepper**

1 Heat the oil in a frying pan and fry the chicken until no longer pink. Add the mushrooms and fry for 30 seconds. Add the spinach and take the pan off the heat. The heat from the pan will cause the spinach to wilt.

2 Preheat the grill.

3 Spread the chicken, mushrooms and spinach evenly among the 6 tortillas. Sprinkle the cheese over and wrap them up (see photo). Place on a large baking tray. Brush the top of each one with a little oil.

4 Place under the grill for 2–3 minutes, or until the quesadilla is browned.

5 Mix the salsa ingredients together and serve with the quesadillas and guacamole.

BEN & NICOLE: "Who would have thought I'd like spinach? Turns out I do. This is why I love this book; it's opened my eyes to new food combos I wouldn't normally have tried."

ONE-POT SAUSAGE MEATBALLS

You can stretch this to serve more people by adding another ½ mug of rice, 1 mug of water and more mushrooms.

500g **sausage meat**

1 tablespoon **olive oil**

1 **onion**, finely chopped

2 cloves **garlic**, finely chopped

6 **mushrooms**, sliced

1 mug (250g) **basmati rice**

2 mugs (600ml) **water**

1 **vegetable stock cube**

400g tin **chopped tomatoes**

1 teaspoon **cumin**

1 teaspoon **ground coriander**

1 tablespoon **tomato purée**

1 tablespoon freshly chopped **coriander** (optional)

1 Cut the sausage meat into 16 and form balls from the portions. Heat the oil in a wok, or large pan, and fry on a medium heat until they are browned and cooked through. Take them out of the pan and set to one side until needed.

2 Add the onions and garlic to the pan and fry until the onions soften a little. Add the mushrooms and fry for 30 seconds.

3 Add the rice to the pan, along with the water, stock, tomatoes, cumin, coriander and tomato purée. Bring to the boil and then turn down to simmer, with a lid on, for 12–15 minutes. The rice should be tender, with a lot of the liquid absorbed.

4 Return the sausage balls to the pan and cook for 3–4 minutes.

5 Serve with the fresh coriander sprinkled over.

£1.28 /PERSON · SERVES 4 · EASE ★★★☆☆ · PREP 25 MINS · COOK 25 MINS · OK TO FREEZE ❄ · GF OPTION

CHICKEN NUGGETS AND WEDGES

Kids love chicken nuggets. The problem is that they can cost a fortune and aren't going to be particularly healthy. This recipe helps to make sure that you know exactly what they are eating and it won't break the bank.

4 large **potatoes**, cut into wedges

1 tablespoon **olive oil**

2 **eggs**

2 tablespoons **flour** (GF option)

3 slices **bread** (GF option), made into breadcrumbs

1 tablespoon freshly chopped **basil** or 1 teaspoon **dried basil**

1 mug (50g) finely grated **Cheddar cheese**

3 **chicken breasts**, cut into strips,

green veg, **broccoli** or **green beans**

tomato sauce or **mayo**

1 Preheat the oven to 200°C fan/220°C/gas 7.

2 Put the potatoes on a baking tray. Sprinkle with oil and salt and pepper. Using your hands, distribute the oil evenly over the potatoes. Put in the oven for 25–30 minutes.

3 Beat the eggs and place in a bowl. Add the flour to the bowl and mix well.

4 Mix together the breadcrumbs, basil and cheese. Use a food processor if you have one.

5 Dip the pieces of chicken in the flour and the egg and then, one by one, in the breadcrumb mixture, coating each piece evenly. Place on a large, greased tray, leaving space between each one. Pile any extra breadcrumbs over the top of each one.

6 Place in the oven for 20 minutes. The chicken nuggets should be nicely browned.

7 While the chicken and potatoes are in the oven, put the greens on to cook.

LUKE & RACHEL: "Samantha and Melody are big fans of chicken nuggets and really love these! They were great finger food when Melody was being weaned and I know it was all good stuff in them for her."

BUDGET DAYS

End of the month, not much left in the piggy bank, so need to stretch things a little? Here we have some inexpensive meals that you and your family will enjoy.

CUMBERLAND HOT DOGS WITH TOMATO SALSA

6 **Cumberland sausages** (GF option)

bread rolls (GF option)

3 tablespoons **soured cream**

TOMATO SALSA

1 tablespoon **olive oil**

4 **tomatoes**, chopped

½ **fat red chilli**, deseeded and finely chopped

1 clove **garlic**, finely chopped

1 tablespoon freshly chopped **basil**, or 1 teaspoon **dried basil**

1 teaspoon **granulated sugar**

1 tablespoon **tomato purée**

1 tablespoon **red wine vinegar**

1 Preheat the oven to 180°C fan/200°C/gas 6. Place the sausages on a tray in the oven and cook for 25 minutes, or until brown.

2 Meanwhile, make the salsa. Heat the oil in a frying pan and add the tomatoes, chilli and garlic. Fry for 1 minute to heat through. Add the rest of the salsa ingredients and heat through. Season. Leave to cool.

3 Cut the bread rolls almost in half, add the sausage and serve with the salsa and soured cream.

£ 0.91 /PERSON | SERVES 4 | EASE ★★☆☆☆ | PREP 15 MINS | COOK 20 MINS | OK TO FREEZE | GF OPTION

MASALA MINCE

2 tablespoons **olive oil**

1 **onion**, sliced

1 clove **garlic**, finely chopped

1 **fat red chilli**, chopped (less if you have young children)

1 tablespoon freshly grated **ginger**

500g **minced beef**

400g tin **chopped tomatoes**

1 tablespoon **tomato purée**

1 **beef stock cube** (GF option)

2 teaspoons **garam masala**

2 tablespoons freshly chopped **coriander**

basmati rice with **pilau seasoning**

1 Heat the oil in a large saucepan or wok. Add the onions and garlic, chilli and ginger. Fry until the onions begin to soften.

2 Add the mince and fry until no longer pink.

3 Add the rest of the ingredients, apart from the coriander and rice. Bring to the boil and then turn down to simmer for 20 minutes. Season well.

4 10 minutes before the end of the cooking time, put the rice on to cook, see p20.

5 Serve with the cooked rice, coriander and some mango chutney (optional).

COURGETTE FRITTERS WITH FETA SALAD

SALAD DRESSING

juice of a **lemon**

1 tablespoon **extra virgin olive oil**

1 teaspoon **granulated sugar**

salt and **pepper**

FETA AND TOMATO SALAD

1 **Little Gem lettuce**

8cm **cucumber**, cut into sticks

2 **spring onions**, cut into thin strips

6–8 **cherry tomatoes**, halved

1 tablespoon **pine nuts**

200g **feta cheese**, crumbled

FRITTERS

4 **eggs**

1 mug (200g) **self-raising flour** (GF option)

3 **courgettes**, grated

2 **spring onions**, grated

200g tin **sweetcorn**, drained

1 Mix the salad dressing ingredients together.

2 Put the eggs in a bowl and beat together with the flour and salt and pepper.

3 Squeeze out any excess liquid from the grated onion and courgettes. Add to the egg mixture along with the sweetcorn. Season well.

4 Heat a little oil in a frying pan and add 1 tablespoon of the fritter mix. You can cook 3 or 4 at a time. Continue until all the fritter mix is used up.

5 Sprinkle the dressing over the salad and serve with the fritters.

PETER & BERNICE: "The feta, pine nuts and the quick and simple dressing gives the salad a fresh, tangy flavour and great texture. Hot fritters and cold salad works surprisingly well together, and the whole meal looks really tempting

£1.35 /PERSON · SERVES 4 · EASE ★★☆☆☆ · PREP 20 MINS · COOK 60 MINS · OK TO FREEZE ❄

ONE-POT CHICKEN HOT POT

If you have one, use a food processor for the potato slices.

1 tablespoon **olive oil**

1 **onion**, sliced

2 cloves **garlic**, chopped

8 boneless **chicken thighs**, cut into bite-sized pieces

1 tablespoon **flour**

4 **carrots**, diced

2 **sweet potatoes**, peeled and cubed

1 mug (150g) defrosted **frozen peas**

1 teaspoon **mixed dried herbs**

1 **chicken stock cube**

1 tablespoon **HP sauce**

1½ mugs (450ml) **water**

4 large **potatoes**, thinly sliced

1 Preheat the oven to 180°C fan/200°C/gas 6.

2 Heat the oil in a large hob-to-oven casserole dish. Add the onion and garlic and fry until the onion begins to soften.

3 Add the chicken and cook until no longer pink. Sprinkle over with flour and mix.

4 Add the carrots, sweet potato, peas, mixed herbs, stock, HP sauce and water. Bring to the boil. Season well.

5 Take off the heat and arrange the sliced potatoes over the top of the chicken mix. Season well.

6 Put a lid on the casserole and place in the oven for 30 minutes. Take the lid off and cook for a further 30 minutes, or until the potatoes are browned.

CORNED BEEF HASH WITH POACHED EGGS

Leaving the hash to brown on the pan is vital to getting lots of flavour from all the crunchy bits.

4 large **potatoes**, cut into chunks

1 tablespoon **olive oil**

25g **butter** (measure using packet)

1 **onion**, sliced

1 **yellow pepper**, chopped

1 teaspoon **paprika**

350g tin **corned beef**, cut into cubes

4 **eggs**

1 tablespoon freshly chopped **parsley**

1 Put the potatoes in boiling, salted water and simmer for 10 minutes. Drain and return to the pan.

2 Heat the oil and butter in a wok and fry the onion and pepper, until they begin to brown. Add the paprika and season well with salt and pepper.

3 Add the potatoes and corned beef to the pan. Leave to fry for 2 minutes, until the stuff on the bottom begins to brown. Stir up the brown bits, then leave for another 2 minutes. Stir up the brown bits from the bottom. Don't keep stirring all the time, allow things to brown.

4 Poach the eggs (see video link below).

5 Serve the eggs on top of the hash and sprinkle with the parsley.

WATCH A VIDEO OF POACHING EGGS AT
NOSHBOOKS.COM/POACHING-EGGS

£0.84 /PERSON · SERVES 4 · EASE ★★★☆☆ · PREP 20 MINS · COOK 30 MINS · OK TO FREEZE · V

CRISPY TOPPED VEGETABLE BAKE

1 tablespoon **olive oil**

1 **red onion**, chopped

1 **red pepper**, chopped

1 clove **garlic**, finely chopped

2 tablespoons **Worcestershire sauce**

1 mug (250g) **basmati rice**, cooked with 2 mugs (600ml) **water**, see p20

8 **mushrooms**, sliced

4 large **tomatoes**, chopped

4 **eggs**

2 slices **wholemeal bread**, made into breadcrumbs

1 teaspoon **dried mixed herbs**, or 1 tablespoon freshly chopped **basil**

1 mug (75g) grated **Cheddar cheese**

1   Preheat the oven to 180°C fan/200°C/gas 6. Grease a large casserole dish.

2   Heat the oil in a wok and fry the onion, peppers and garlic. Once browned, add the Worcestershire sauce and mix together.

3   Add the cooked rice, mushrooms and tomatoes to the wok. Season well with salt and pepper and mix gently. Place in the casserole dish.

4   Make 4 hollows in the rice and break an egg into each one.

5   Mix together the breadcrumbs, herbs and cheese. Sprinkle over the top and place in the oven for 30 minutes. The top should be browned a little. If your children are older, you can replace the Cheddar with Parmesan.

£ 1.97 /PERSON · SERVES 4 · EASE ★★★☆☆ · PREP 25 MINS · GF OPTION

SMOKED SALMON AND CREAM CHEESE SPAGHETTI

spaghetti, see p21 (GF option)

1 tablespoon **olive oil**

2 medium **courgettes**, thinly sliced

6 **spring onions**, chopped

200g pack **smoked salmon trimmings**

300g pack **cream cheese with garlic and herbs**

zest and juice of a **lemon**

1 Put the spaghetti on to boil and simmer for 5–6 minutes.

2 Heat the oil in a wok and add the courgettes. Fry for 1–2 minutes until they begin to soften.

3 Add the onions, salmon and cream cheese to the pan and cook until everything is heated through. This will take 2 minutes max. Add the lemon juice and zest.

4 Drain the spaghetti, but retain the cooking liquid.

5 Add the spaghetti to the wok along with a little of the spaghetti water. Mix together.

6 Serve straight away.

£0.87 /PERSON · SERVES 4 · EASE ★★★☆☆ · PREP 25 MINS · COOK 40 MINS · OK TO FREEZE ❄ · GF OPTION

BEEF AND MUSHROOM PIE WITH CRISPY POTATO TOP

Ovens vary slightly, so make sure you leave this in the oven until the potatoes are nice and crispy on top.

2 tablespoons **olive oil**

1 **onion**, roughly chopped

1 clove **garlic**, finely chopped

500g **minced beef**

1 tablespoon **flour**
(GF option)

400g tin **chopped tomatoes**

250g **mushrooms**, sliced

1 tablespoon **tomato purée**

1 teaspoon **granulated sugar**

1 teaspoon **dried mixed herbs**

1 mug (300ml) **water**

1 **beef stock cube**
(GF option)

3–4 medium **potatoes**

1 Preheat the oven to 180°C fan/200°C/gas 6.

2 Heat 1 tablespoon of the oil in a frying pan and fry the onion and garlic for 2 minutes.

3 Add the mince and cook until no longer pink.

4 Add the flour and stir well.

5 Add the tomatoes, mushrooms, tomato purée, sugar, herbs, water and stock. Bring to the boil for the sauce to thicken. Leave to simmer for 10 minutes.

6 If you have a food processor, grate the potatoes on the most coarse setting, or just use the coarse setting on a cheese grater. No need to peel the potatoes. Squeeze out the excess liquid from the potatoes, place in a large bowl and add the other tablespoon of oil, together with plenty of salt and pepper. Mix together.

7 Put the mince mixture into the casserole dish and spread the potatoes over the top, as loosely as you can, as the heat needs to get to them all. Place in the oven for 35–40 minutes, until the potatoes are cooked and browned on top.

BEN & NICOLE: "If you have a food processor, doing the potato top is so quick. It makes a delicious crunchy crust."

£ 1.07 /PERSON · SERVES 4 · EASE ★★☆☆☆ · PREP 25 MINS · COOK 50 MINS · OK TO FREEZE ❄ · GF OPTION

SAUSAGE AND VEG TRAYBAKE

You can also add carrots, courgettes or tomatoes to the roast veg. This is a good way to use up the veg left in the fridge at the end of the week.

ONE MORE THING: Also can add ½ teaspoon paprika to the tomato sauce to spice it up, if you like.

WHERE ON EARTH: White wine vinegar is usually near the 'frozen section', with the 'regular' vinegars.

8-12 **fat sausages**
(GF option)

4 medium **potatoes**, cut into chunks

1 **red onion**, cut into wedges

2 **parsnips**, cut into long strips

2 **sweet potatoes**, cut into chunks

2 tablespoons **olive oil**

1 sprig **fresh rosemary** or
1 teaspoon **dried rosemary**

PIQUANT TOMATO SAUCE

1 tablespoon **olive oil**

1 **onion**, sliced

400g tin **chopped tomatoes**

1 teaspoon **black pepper**

1 tablespoon **tomato purée**

1 tablespoon **white wine vinegar**

1 teaspoon **granulated sugar**

1　Preheat the oven to 180°C fan/200°C/gas 6.

2　Put the sausages and vegetables into a roasting tray, drizzle with the oil and distribute it with your hands. Season well with salt and pepper and sprinkle some rosemary over the top. Put in the oven for 45-50 minutes.

3　While everything is roasting, make the tomato sauce. Heat the oil in a saucepan, add the onions and fry until soft. Add the rest of the ingredients and bring to the boil. Simmer for 2-3 minutes. Blitz with a hand-held blender.

LUKE & RACHEL: "Very easy. I love meals you can prepare during nap times and put in the oven when you want."

ORIENTAL EGG AND SMOKED SALMON BAKE

Smoked salmon has quite a strong taste, so the small quantity here will provide enough flavour. The trimmings are very economical and can be frozen, so it's really handy to keep some in the freezer.

1 mug (250g) **basmati rice**, cooked in 2 mugs (600ml) **water**

200g **smoked salmon trimmings**

6 **spring onions**, chopped

1 tablespoon **toasted sesame oil**

2 tablespoons **soy sauce** (GF option)

6 **eggs**, beaten

½ mug (150ml) **soured cream**

1 mug (75g) grated **Cheddar cheese**

salad to serve

1 Preheat the oven to 200°C fan/220°C/gas 7. Grease a shallow casserole dish.

2 Put the rice on to cook, see p20. Pour the rice into the casserole dish.

3 Add the salmon and spring onions and distribute evenly. Season well with salt and pepper.

4 Add the sesame oil and soy to the beaten eggs and gently stir. Pour into the casserole dish.

5 Spoon the soured cream over the top and then sprinkle the cheese over.

6 Place in the oven for 15–20 minutes until the cheese bubbles and begins to go brown.

7 Serve with salad.

DAVID & HANNAH: "This would not be a recipe I'd normally choose myself, but I was surprised how tasty it was. I loved that it was so easy to make and good value. I will do it again."

   V GF OPTION

CHEESE AND ONION PATTIES WITH APPLE CHUTNEY

4 medium **potatoes**, cut into small chunks

1 tablespoon **olive oil**

5 slices **wholemeal bread** (GF option), made into breadcrumbs

1¾ mugs (130g) grated **Cheddar cheese**

3 **spring onions**, chopped

2 sprigs **fresh thyme**, leaves only

1 tablespoon freshly chopped **parsley**

3 **eggs**

APPLE CHUTNEY

1 tablespoon **olive oil**

1 **onion**, chopped

1 **eating apple**, cored and chopped

1 tablespoon **soy sauce** (GF option)

1 tablespoon **white wine vinegar**

1½ tablespoons **honey**

2 tablespoons **water**

1 Preheat the oven to 180°C fan/200°C/gas 6.

2 Put the potatoes on a baking tray, sprinkle with the oil, season well and distribute well with your hands. Put in the oven for 30-35 minutes.

3 Mix together the breadcrumbs, cheese, spring onions, thyme and parsley.

4 Add 2 eggs and one egg yolk. Season well and mix together.

5 Turn out onto a board and form 8 small patties. Place on a greased baking tray and put in the oven, with the potatoes, for 20 minutes.

6 To make the chutney, heat the oil in a saucepan and fry the onions, until they begin to brown a little. Add the rest of the ingredients and simmer gently for 5 minutes. Set to one side until needed.

7 Serve the patties with the mini roasts and the chutney.

PETER & BERNICE: "This quick meal is bursting with a variety of textures and flavours. The patties are crunchy on the outside and soft on the inside and the tangy apple chutney is a great flavour contrast. Mini roasts taste much better than chips, and are healthier as you leave the skins on and you don't need lots of oil to cook them. We have thyme growing in our garden, and usually the other ingredients are to hand, so this is a brilliant recipe for those 'arrgh, nothing planned for tea' moments. Guaranteed clean plates all round."

£0.73 /PERSON · SERVES 4 · EASE ★★★☆☆ · PREP 30 MINS · OK TO FREEZE · GF OPTION

SAUSAGE STEW WITH BORLOTTI BEANS

Try experimenting with different flavoured sausages to change the taste.

1 tablespoon **olive oil**

8 thick **sausages** (GF option)

1 **onion**, sliced

1 clove **garlic**, chopped

4 **tomatoes**, chopped

1 tablespoon **tomato purée**

1 **vegetable stock cube** (GF option)

2 mugs (600ml) **water**

1 teaspoon **mixed herbs**

1 pinch **chilli flakes**

1 portion **spaghetti**, broken into pieces (GF option)

400g tin **borlotti beans**, rinsed and drained

1 Heat the oil in a wok and fry the sausages until they are browned on the outside and cooked through. Take out of the pan and leave to one side until needed.

2 Add the onions and garlic to the wok and fry until the onions begin to soften.

3 Add the tomatoes and fry for 1 minute.

4 Add the tomato purée, stock, water, herbs, chilli and the broken spaghetti. Cut each sausage into 4 and return to the pan. Bring to the boil and then turn down to simmer, with the lid on, for 4-5 minutes, or until the spaghetti is cooked. Add more water if necessary.

5 Add the beans and cook for 1 minute, or until the beans are heated through.

DAVID & HANNAH: "This was very easy and quick to make, the kids and I really enjoyed it. I like the little kick the chilli flakes give it."

PASTITSIO

If you have a food processor, use it for the breadcrumbs and then change the attachment and grate the cheese straight in. Very quick, no fuss.

1 tablespoon **olive oil**

1 **onion**, chopped

2 cloves **garlic**, chopped

500g **minced beef**

400g tin **chopped tomatoes**

1 tablespoon **tomato purée**

1 **beef stock cube**

2 mugs (200g) **pasta** (we used penne)

2 heaped tablespoons **flour**

50g **butter** (measure using packet)

2 mugs (600ml) **milk**

2 slices **wholemeal bread**, made into breadcrumbs

1 tablespoon freshly chopped **basil**, or 1 teaspoon **dried basil**

1 mug (75g) grated **Cheddar cheese**

1 Heat the oil in a wok, or large pan, and fry the onion and garlic until it begins to brown.

2 Add the meat to the pan and fry until it is no longer pink.

3 Add the tomatoes, tomato purée and stock. Bring to the boil, then turn down to simmer for 10 minutes. Season well with salt and pepper.

4 Put the pasta on to cook, see p21. Drain and leave until needed.

5 Heat the oven to 180°C fan/200°C/gas 6. Grease a casserole dish.

6 Make the sauce by putting the flour and butter in a pan. Heat and stir until it forms a paste. Gradually stir in, or whisk the milk, until you have a creamy consistency. Gently bring to the boil and cook for 30 seconds. Season well with salt and pepper.

7 Put the pasta on the bottom of the casserole dish and press down. Pour the meat sauce over and spread. Pour the white sauce over the top.

8 Mix together the breadcrumbs, basil and grated cheese and sprinkle over the top. Place in the oven for 20–25 minutes until the top is browned and crispy.

JOE & SARAH: "Joe's parents own an Italian Deli, so we eat pasta quite often, but I have never cooked pasta as a bake. I invited the family over the day I tried this and it was pleasing to see all the plates mopped up and squeaky clean. Yippee, less washing up for me!"

CAKES & COOKIES

We all need a treat every now and then. Some of these cakes and cookies are downright naughty, whilst others have a hint of 'healthy' about them. Heather, another of my amazing testers, made the 'Apricot Flap Jacks' and convinced herself that they must be good for her as they had oats, seeds and dried fruit in them, despite the syrup and sugar. Her imagination could not convince her of the same when it came to test the 'Millionaire's Shortbread'! Both went down really well with her family. There are some lunch-box cookies which will work out much cheaper than cereal bars.

 £4.66 /TOTAL MAKES 18 EASE ★★☆☆☆ PREP 15 MINS COOK 25 MINS OK TO FREEZE ❄ V

DATE AND NUT BARS

½ mug (105g) **brown sugar**

½ mug (85g) **self-raising flour**

½ mug (60g) **oats**

1 teaspoon **mixed spice**

250g **ready-to-eat dates**, chopped

1 mug (100g) **pecan nuts**, chopped

2 **eggs**

⅓ mug (100ml) **vegetable oil**

1 Preheat the oven to 160°C fan/180°C/gas 5. Grease and line a 20x30cm baking tray.

2 Mix the dry ingredients together in a bowl.

3 Beat the eggs, mix in the oil and add to the dry ingredients. Mix well.

4 Press into the baking tray and place in the oven for 25 minutes.

5 Leave to cool and cut into approx. 18 pieces.

STEVE & CANDY: "I love the fact that it has got mug measures. I really enjoy the mixed spice flavour."

£2.42 /TOTAL · MAKES 20 · EASE ★★☆☆☆ · PREP 20 MINS · COOK 12 MINS · OK TO FREEZE ❄ · V

ORANGE COOKIES

180g softened **butter** (measure using packet)

½ mug (130g) **granulated sugar**

2 **egg** yolks

1 teaspoon **vanilla extract**

zest of an **orange**

1¼ mugs (230g) **self-raising flour**

1 mug (160g) **icing sugar**

juice of an **orange**

sprinkles

1 Preheat the oven to 180°C fan/200°C/gas 6. Grease 2 baking trays.

2 Cream the butter and sugar together. Add the egg yolks and the vanilla. Mix well.

3 Stir in the orange zest and then the flour. Mix to a stiff dough.

4 Make 20 small balls and place them on the trays. Give them a squash down.

5 Place in the oven for 12 minutes until slightly browned.

6 Once cooled, mix the icing sugar and enough orange juice together to make a fairly stiff icing. Put a blob on each cookie and then shake over with a few sprinkles.

 £3.80 /TOTAL
 MAKES 24
 EASE ★★☆☆☆
 PREP 20 MINS
 COOK 45 MINS
 OK TO FREEZE
 V

CARROT CAKE TRAYBAKE

You can make this recipe into small buns, it makes about 24. Put in bun cases and bake in the oven for 25 minutes. Makes good lunch box additions.

4 **eggs**

1 mug (210g) **soft brown sugar**

2/3 mug (165ml) **sunflower oil**

1 3/4 mugs (340g) **self-raising flour**

1 1/2 teaspoon **ground cinnamon**

4 medium **carrots**, grated

zest and juice of an **orange**

TOPPING

300g pack **cream cheese**

50g **butter** (measure using packet)

3/4 mug (125g) **icing sugar**

1 teaspoon grated **orange rind**

1 Preheat the oven to 160°C fan/180°C/gas 4. Grease and line a 20x30cm cake tin.

2 Separate the eggs and beat the whites to a soft peak.

3 In a separate bowl, whisk the egg yolks together with the sugar until they go pale.

4 Gradually add the oil, whisking all the time.

5 Add the flour, cinnamon, carrots, zest and juice of the orange. Mix gently together.

6 Gently add the egg whites and mix well.

7 Pour into the cake tin and bake in the oven for 40–45 minutes.

8 To make the topping simply mix the ingredients together and leave in the fridge until needed. Do not over mix, as the cream cheese will go runny.

9 Once the cake is cooled, spread the topping over.

GARY & NIKKI: "This is the best carrot cake I have ever tried. The family gave it 10/10."

£ 4.11 /TOTAL · MAKES 12 · EASE ★★☆☆☆ · PREP 20 MINS · COOK 40 MINS · OK TO FREEZE · V

BANANA AND PECAN NUT CAKE

150g softened **butter** (measure using packet)

³⁄₄ mug (140g) **soft brown sugar**

2 **eggs**

3 ripe **bananas**, crushed

½ mug (50g) **pecan nuts**, chopped roughly

⅓ mug (125g) **raisins**

1⅓ mugs (280g) **self-raising flour**

2 tablespoons **marmalade**

½ x 100g packet **flaked almonds**

1 Preheat the oven to 180°C fan/200°C/gas 6. Grease and line a 20x30cm baking tray.

2 Beat the butter and sugar until soft and creamy.

3 Add the eggs, one at a time, together with the bananas, and beat well.

4 Add the chopped nuts, raisins and flour. Fold in until well mixed, but do not beat.

5 Pour into the cake tin and spread evenly. Place in the oven for 35–40 minutes. The cake should be nicely browned and bounce back when pressed.

6 Gently heat the marmalade in a pan. Brush over the top of the warm cake. Sprinkle with the almonds.

£ 4.27 /TOTAL · MAKES 20 · EASE ★★☆☆☆ · PREP 20 MINS · COOK 15 MINS · OK TO FREEZE · V

LUNCH BOX COOKIES

250g **butter**, softened

3/4 mug (170g) **brown sugar**

2 **eggs**

3/4 mug (170g) **self-raising flour**

11/2 mugs (185g) **oats**

1/3 mug (50g) **raisins**

1/2 mug (50g) **desiccated coconut**

1 mug (200g) **ready-to-eat dried apricots**, finely chopped

1   Preheat the oven to 180°C fan/200°C/gas 6.

2   Beat the butter and sugar until light and fluffy.

3   Add the eggs, one at a time, and beat again.

4   Add the rest of the ingredients and mix.

5   Place dessertspoons of the dough on greased baking trays and flatten down a little. Place in the oven for 12–15 minutes, until they are golden brown. They will still be a little soft in the centre. If you want more crispy biscuits, leave them in the oven for another 5 minutes.

£2.82 /TOTAL · MAKES 20 · EASE ★★☆☆☆ · PREP 25 MINS · COOK 10 MINS · OK TO FREEZE · V

CHOCOLATE OAT COOKIES

225g **butter** (measure using packet), melted

1 rounded tablespoon **golden syrup**

1½ mugs (185g) **oats**

½ mug (135g) **granulated sugar**

1 mug (170g) **self-raising flour**

½ x 100g packet **chocolate chips**

100g melted **chocolate** to decorate

1 Preheat the oven to 180°C fan/200°C/gas 6. Grease 2 large baking trays.

2 Melt the butter and syrup in a pan.

3 Put the oats, sugar, flour and chocolate chips in a large bowl and mix together. Add the butter and syrup and mix well.

4 Place dessertspoons of the mixture on the trays, but set well apart, as they will spread to about 8cm. Press down the centres.

5 Place in the oven for 8–10 minutes, until they just begin to brown on the outsides. The centres will still appear a bit soft.

6 Once cooled, drizzle over the melted chocolate.

BEN & NICOLE: "Really easy. The kids loved them. I even overcooked them and they were still great."

MILLIONAIRE'S SHORTBREAD

Scoring the chocolate, when it is half-set, stops it cracking when you come to cut the cookies at the end.

BASE

200g **butter** (measure using packet)

1/3 mug (80g) **caster sugar**

1 1/2 mugs (300g) **plain flour**

CARAMEL

50g **butter** (measure using packet)

1/3 mug (90g) **granulated sugar**

400g tin **condensed milk**

2 tablespoons **golden syrup**

TOPPING

200g bar **milk chocolate**

100g bar **white chocolate**

1 Preheat the oven to 180°C fan/200°C/gas 6. Grease and line a baking tray.

2 Cream the butter and sugar. Add the flour and mix together. Press into the baking tray and place in the oven for 12–15 minutes.

3 Put the caramel ingredients in a saucepan and gently heat. Bring to the boil and stir frequently. Simmer gently for 5–8 minutes until it turns golden brown. Leave to cool a little then pour over the shortbread. Leave to set for about 1 hour.

4 Melt the chocolate in a bowl over a pan of simmering water.

5 Spread the chocolate over the caramel, milk chocolate first, followed by the white chocolate drizzled over the top. Leave in the fridge for 45 mins. Score the top of the chocolate, as if you were going to cut it.

6 Return to the fridge until the chocolate has completely set. Cut into squares and hide it from any chocoholics!

ANDY & HEATHER:
"Absolutely yummy, the family loved these."

WATCH A VIDEO OF HOW TO DO FEATHERING AT
NOSHBOOKS.COM/FEATHERING

£4.35 /TOTAL · MAKES 25 · EASE ★★★☆☆ · PREP 20 MINS · COOK 10 MINS · OK TO FREEZE ❄ · V

COFFEE SHOP COOKIES

This is a good one to do with small children. One good way to soften butter is to let the child squish the butter with their freshly washed hands. Works wonders and they love it.

ONE MORE THING: Try playing around with the oven timing to get the perfect cookie, as all ovens vary a little.

100g **butter** (measure using packet)

1¼ mugs (260g) **soft brown sugar**

½ x 375g pot of **Nutella**

1 teaspoon **vanilla extract**

1 **egg**

1 mug (170g) **self-raising flour**

1 tablespoon **cocoa**

½ x 100g packet **chocolate chips**

½ mug (50g) **pecan nuts,** chopped

white chocolate to decorate

1 Preheat the oven to 180°C fan/200°C/gas 6. Grease or line a couple of baking trays.

2 Cream together the butter and sugar.

3 Add the Nutella, vanilla and egg and beat well.

4 Add the flour, cocoa, chocolate chips and pecans. Mix well.

5 Put dessertspoons of the mixture well apart on the trays. They will spread quite a lot and make quite thin cookies.

6 Bake for 12 minutes in the oven. They will look as though they are not cooked, but when left to cool, will be crunchy on the outside and chewy in the centre.

7 Once cooled, drizzle with a bit of melted white chocolate.

JOE & SARAH: "These are delicious. They did not even last the day before they were gone."

WATCH A VIDEO OF HOW TO MELT CHOCOLATE AT
NOSHBOOKS.COM/MELTING-CHOCOLATE

MELTING MOMENTS

175g **butter** (measure using packet), softened

⅓ mug (60g) **icing sugar**

1 mug (200g) **plain flour**

½ mug (60g) **cornflour**

1 teaspoon **vanilla extract**

FILLING

125g **butter** (measure using packet), softened

1 mug (185g) **icing sugar**

1 teaspoon **vanilla extract**

1 Heat the oven to 160°C fan/180°C/gas 4. Grease a baking tray.

2 Beat the butter and icing sugar together.

3 Add the flour, cornflour and vanilla extract and beat, until the mixture holds together.

4 Flour a board and cut the mixture into 32 pieces. Roll into balls and place on the baking tray. They will not spread too much, so can be fairly close together. Press a fork onto the tops of the dough balls and squash down a little. This makes a pretty mark.

5 Place in the oven for 10–12 minutes, until very slightly browned. Leave to cool.

6 Make the filling by beating the ingredients together. Once the cookies are cooled, sandwich them together with the filling. Dust the tops with icing sugar.

APRICOT FLAP JACKS

125g **butter** (measure using packet)

½ mug (105g) **soft brown sugar**

3 rounded tablespoons **golden syrup**

2 mugs (240g) **oats** (GF option)

½ x 100g packet **pumpkin seeds**

½ mug or 12 **ready-to-eat-dried apricots**, chopped

1 Heat the oven to 160°C fan/180°C/gas 4. Line a 20x30cm baking tray.

2 Put the butter, sugar and syrup in a saucepan and gently heat, until everything is melted and the sugar dissolved.

3 Put the oats, seeds and apricots in a large bowl. Stir in the syrup mixture and mix until you cannot see any dry oats.

4 Press into the baking tray and flatten out with a palette knife. Place in the oven for 20-25 minutes. The top should be browned a little.

5 Leave to cool and cut into bars. This should make good lunch box fillers.

£2.56 /TOTAL · MAKES 16 · EASE ★★☆☆☆ · PREP 15 MINS · COOK 10 MINS · OK TO FREEZE · V

CHOCOLATE CHIP COOKIES

Don't skimp on the butter and use margarine instead, it won't taste nearly as good!

ONE MORE THING: You can freeze the mixture, so that you can defrost and cook at a later date.

125g softened **butter** (measure using packet)

1 mug (210g) **soft brown sugar**

1 large **egg**

1 teaspoon **vanilla** extract

100g **white chocolate chips**

1¼ mugs (225g) **self-raising flour**. Take out 1 tablespoon and replace with 1 tablespoon **cocoa**

1   Preheat the oven to 180°C fan/200°C/gas 6. Grease 2 baking trays.

2   Mix the butter and sugar together and beat well. Add the egg and the vanilla extract. Beat well.

3   Add the chocolate chips and mix, then add the flour and mix well. The cookie dough will be quite stiff. Tip onto a floured surface and squash into a long sausage. Do not knead the dough; in fact, handle it as little as possible. Cut into 16 and roll each portion into a ball. Squash each ball until it is about 1.5cm thick and approximately 6cm across. Place on the baking tray.

4   Put in the oven and bake for 10–12 minutes. The cookies do not need to brown, just be crisp on the outside. Leave to cool for a few minutes.

DAVID & HANNAH: "These cookies are great and very easy to do with the kids. Very quick and not too messy! My girls had one in their school lunch boxes and thought they were yummy."

MUFFINS

2²/₃ mugs (525g) **self-raising flour**

1 mug (175g) **brown** or **granulated sugar**

2 **eggs**, beaten

1½ mugs (450ml) **milk**

³/₄ mug (225ml) **vegetable oil**

muffin cases

1 Preheat oven to 180°C fan/200°C/gas 6.

2 Mix all the dry ingredients together, then add the wet ones. It will be a bit lumpy and quite 'wet'.

3 Fill 18 large muffin cases and bake in the oven for 25 minutes. If you use smaller bun cases, you will only need to bake them for 20 minutes.

VARIATIONS

CHOCOLATE CHIP MUFFINS

Add two 100g packets of chocolate chips. Two different varieties work well; for example, white and milk chocolate. If you want double choc chip muffins, instead of the 3 mugs of flour, use 2²/₃ flour and ¹/₃ mug drinking chocolate.

RASPBERRY OR BLUEBERRY MUFFINS

Take ³/₄ x 400g bag of defrosted frozen fruit, drain away the liquid and add the fruit to the wet ingredients.

APPLE CINNAMON MUFFINS

Add 1 mug of finely chopped apple to the wet ingredients and 2 teaspoons ground cinnamon to the dry ingredients.

BANANA AND NUT MUFFINS

Add 1 mug of mashed, ripe banana and 1 mug of chopped nuts (cashews, Brazils, pecans or walnuts) along with the wet ingredients.

CHOCOLATE AND MAPLE MUFFINS

Add ¹/₂ mug maple syrup to the wet ingredients and 200g chocolate (white or milk), chopped into chunks, to the dry ingredients.

£0.24 /PERSON | MAKES 12 | EASE ★★★☆☆ | PREP 20 MINS | COOK 20 MINS | OK TO FREEZE | V

BUTTERFLY CAKES

If you wish, you can add colouring to the icing and put sprinkles on the top. If you want to make chocolate cakes, replace a tablespoon of the four with a tablespoon of cocoa and add ½ teaspoon baking powder.

ONE MORE THING: These are great for kids' parties.

170g softened **butter** (measure using packet)

²/₃ mug (160g) **caster sugar**

3 **eggs**

1 teaspoon **vanilla extract**

1 mug (170g) **self-raising flour**

12 **bun cases**

100g softened **butter** (measure using packet)

1 mug (185g) **icing sugar**

1 Preheat the oven to 180°C fan/200°C/gas 6. Put the bun cases in the bun tins.

2 Beat the sugar and butter until smooth. To make life easier, use a food mixer or processor.

3 Add the eggs, one at a time, and the vanilla extract. Beat until light in colour.

4 Gently fold in the flour, but don't over mix. If the eggs were small, add a tablespoon of water to the mix. Place a heaped dessertspoon in each bun case. Should make 12 cakes.

5 Put in the oven for 15–20 minutes. The cakes should have risen and be golden brown.

6 To make the filling, beat the butter and the icing sugar together.

7 Once the cakes are cooled, cut out a circle from the top of each cake and cut that circle in half. Put a dessertspoon of the butter cream in each cake and place the two halves of the circle to form wings (see photo).

8 Put a tablespoon of icing sugar in a sieve and shake over the cakes.

BEN & NICOLE: "These are surprisingly easy to make and taste fab. The kids love the way they look."

£ 5.18 /TOTAL | MAKES 24 | EASE ★★★☆☆ | PREP 20 MINS | FRIDGE 2 HOURS | OK TO FREEZE | V

ROCKY ROAD

Cut these very small as they are quite rich. They make great treats for a kids' party.

100g **butter** (measured using packet)

225g **plain chocolate**

2 tablespoons **golden syrup**

2 tablespoons **caster sugar**

1 tablespoon **cocoa powder**

100g packet **Maltesers**

100g **white chocolate chips**

100g packet **mini marshmallows**

³/₄ x 300g packet **Hobnobs**, broken up

2 tablespoons **icing sugar**

1 Line a baking tray with greaseproof paper.

2 Gently heat the butter, chocolate, syrup and sugar in a pan, until the sugar crystals disappear. Stir in the cocoa powder and mix until smooth. Leave to cool for 15 minutes.

3 Put the Maltesers, chocolate chips, marshmallows and biscuits in a large mixing-bowl. Once the chocolate has cooled, pour into the bowl and mix everything together.

4 Tip into the baking tray and spread evenly. Place in the fridge for at least 2 hours. Turn out onto a board, sieve a little icing sugar over and cut into small pieces. Keep in the fridge.

ANDY & HEATHER: "These are delicious. Beware, once you start eating them, they are moreish."

WATCH A VIDEO OF MELTING CHOCOLATE AT
NOSHBOOKS.COM/MELTING-CHOCOLATE

YUMMY DESSERTS

These are for special days and treats. We all love a good bit of indulgence and, so long as we don't have them every day, we can feel free to enjoy them. There are one or two old favourites and some new ideas too.

FRUIT CRUMBLE

You can vary the filling. Use 3 apples and make it all apple, or use other frozen or fresh fruits.

2 medium **cooking apples**

¼ mug (75ml) **water**

1 tablespoon **granulated sugar**

500g packet **frozen fruits**, e.g. blueberries and strawberries

1 mug (170g) **plain flour**

100g **butter** (measure using packet)

2 tablespoons **granulated sugar**

1 mug (100g) **muesli**

cream or **custard** to serve

1 Preheat the oven to 180°C fan/200°C/gas 6.

2 Peel and core the apples and cut into bite-sized chunks. Place in a saucepan with water. Bring to the boil and simmer gently for 3–4 minutes, until the apples begin to soften. Add the sugar and frozen fruit and simmer for 1 minute, or until the sugar has dissolved.

3 Pour the mixture into the bottom of an 18cm casserole dish. Set to one side.

4 Rub the butter into the flour with your fingers until it resembles breadcrumbs (use a food processor if you have one). Add the sugar and muesli and mix together.

5 Sprinkle evenly over the top of the fruit and press down gently. Cook in the oven for 20–25 minutes. The top should be golden brown.

**WATCH A VIDEO OF RUBBING BUTTER INTO FLOUR AT
NOSHBOOKS.COM/RUBBING**

JELLY BERRY TRIFLE WITH FRESH STRAWBERRIES

300g **fresh strawberries**

2 **soft trifle sponges**, pulled apart

1 packet **jelly, raspberry** or **strawberry**

2 mugs (600ml) **water**

2 tablespoons **runny honey**

500ml tub **Greek yogurt**

1   Take the tops off the strawberries and cut into bite-sized pieces. Place in the trifle bowl with the sponges.

2   Dissolve the jelly cubes in a mug of boiling water and then add the other 1 mug of cold water.

3   Pour the jelly over the fruit and sponges. Leave in the fridge for 2–3 hours until set.

4   Mix the honey into the yogurt and pour over the set jelly.

RASPBERRY DELIGHT WITH PRALINE SHARDS

1 mug (250g) **granulated sugar**

½ mug (50g) **flaked almonds**

½ x 500g bag **frozen raspberries**

4 ready-made **meringue nests**

300ml **double cream**

1 mug (300ml) **Greek yogurt**

1 Make the praline by putting the sugar in a clean frying pan over a medium heat. Allow it to heat up gently and keep shaking the pan. Do not stir. Eventually the sugar will melt and go golden brown. Add the almonds and quickly spread the praline out onto a Teflon sheet. Allow to cool and then break into shards. Set to one side until needed.

2 Put the raspberries in a bowl and break them up a bit.

3 Break up the meringue nests into chunks, not dust.

4 Whip the double cream until it begins to stiffen. Add the yogurt.

5 Mix everything together, except the praline, and divide into 4–5 bowls. Leave in the fridge for a maximum of 2 hours, any more and the meringues will dissolve. Decorate with praline shards.

LIME AND GINGER CHEESECAKE

You can change the ginger snaps for Hobnobs and the lime for lemon. This makes a wonderfully simple, lemon cheesecake.

ONE MORE THING: An easy way to remove the cake from the tin is to put a can (e.g. can of beans) under the cake tin and gently push down the sides of the cake tin, leaving the cake balanced on the can of beans.

200g **ginger snaps**

100g **butter** (measure using packet), melted

300g pack **cream cheese**

3 heaped tablespoons **icing sugar**

zest and juice of 3 **limes**

300ml **double cream**

1 Put the ginger snaps into a plastic bag and give them a good bash with a rolling pin, until they look like breadcrumbs.

2 Melt the butter and add the biscuit crumbs. Line a 20cm, loose-bottomed cake tin with greaseproof paper. Press the biscuit crumbs into the base.

3 Mix together the cream cheese, sugar, lime juice and rind until it is smooth. Mix with a whisk or electric beater if it goes lumpy.

4 Beat the cream in a separate bowl until it is stiff. Be careful not to make it into butter. Gently mix together with the cheese and lime. The lime juice will cause the cream to set and should begin to go thick as you mix it together.

5 Pour on top of the biscuit base and smooth out.

6 Place in the fridge for 2 hours.

DAVID & HANNAH: "I made this for a bigger group of people and they all enjoyed it. I thought it was delicious and easy to make."

WATCH A VIDEO OF HOW MUCH TO BEAT CREAM AT
NOSHBOOKS.COM/CREAM

BERRY CINNAMON TORTE

If you like cinnamon you will love this. The cream, Greek yogurt and honey make a great alternative to just having cream.

175g **butter** (measure using packet), softened

²/₃ mug (180g) **granulated sugar**

3 **eggs**

1½ mugs (175g) **ground almonds**

1 mug (170g) **self-raising flour**

1 teaspoon ground **cinnamon**

2 tablespoons **water**

½ x 400g packet defrosted **frozen berries** (e.g. summer fruits or raspberries)

icing sugar, for dusting

½ mug (150ml) **double cream**, whipped

½ mug (150ml) **Greek yogurt**

1 tablespoon **honey**

1 Preheat the oven to 180°C fan/200°C/gas 6. Grease and line a 23cm cake tin.

2 Beat the butter and sugar together until light and fluffy. Add the eggs and beat well.

3 Add the almonds, flour, cinnamon and water and mix well.

4 Put half the mixture on the bottom of the cake tin and spread out. Spread the fruit over and then the rest of the torte mixture. It will spread out in the oven, so does not need to be too even.

5 Place in the oven for 40–45 minutes. It should be browned and risen. Once cooled, sift some icing sugar over the top.

6 Mix the cream, yogurt and honey and add to the whipped cream. Serve with the torte.

WATCH A VIDEO OF HOW MUCH TO BEAT CREAM AT
NOSHBOOKS.COM/CREAM

£0.59 /PERSON · SERVES 6 · EASE ★★★★☆ · PREP 25 MINS · COOK 30 MINS · FRIDGE 30 MINS · OK TO FREEZE ❄ · V

APPLE PIE WITH CUSTARD

You can make the pastry in a food processor. Put the flour and butter in the processor and pulse a few times until it looks like breadcrumbs. Add the sugar and pulse once. Add the egg and about 3 tablespoons of water and pulse again. It should make a soft dough. Take out of the processor and squash together. Place in the fridge for ½ an hour.

3 large **Bramley apples**, peeled and cut into chunks

¾ mug (225ml) **water**

3 tablespoons **granulated sugar**

1 teaspoon **mixed spice**

150g **butter** (measure using packet)

1½ mugs (300g) **plain flour**

1 tablespoon **icing sugar**

1 **egg**, beaten

3 tablespoons **water**

1 beaten **egg** to brush the top

2 mugs (600ml) **milk**

2 tablespoons **custard powder**

2 tablespoons **granulated sugar**

1 teaspoon **vanilla extract**

1 Put the apples and the water in a pan and bring to the boil. Turn down to simmer, with a lid on the pan, for 3 minutes. The apples should be a bit 'fluffy' round the edges. Add the sugar and spice and mix. Pour into a pie dish.

2 To make the pastry, rub in the butter and flour until it looks like breadcrumbs. Add the sugar and stir. Add the egg and enough water to make a soft dough. Squash together, cover with cling film and place in the fridge for ½ an hour.

3 Preheat the oven to 180°C fan/200°C/gas 6.

4 Roll the pastry out and place over the apples. Trim the edges and pinch them to look pretty. Brush with the beaten egg and make a hole in the centre to let out the steam. Place in the oven for 25 minutes.

5 If you are making the custard, put the milk on to boil. Mix the custard powder and sugar together in a jug and add a little cold milk to mix it to a thin paste. Once the milk is boiling, add to the jug and stir quickly. If the custard does not thicken, place in the microwave for 30 seconds and then stir. Serve with the pie.

WATCH A VIDEO OF MAKING PASTRY
NOSHBOOKS.COM/PASTRY

QUICK APRICOT AND RASPBERRY TRIFLES

8 **trifle sponge fingers**

juice of an **orange**

400g tin **apricots**, drained and sliced

100g **raspberries**

300ml **custard**

300ml **double cream**

50g **white chocolate**, grated

1 Break up the sponges and place in the bottom of individual dishes. Divide the orange juice between them. Add the apricots and raspberries to the bowls.

2 Divide the custard between the bowls.

3 Whip the cream and place on top. Sprinkle the grated chocolate over the top.

STICKY TOFFEE PUDDING WITH HOT FUDGE SAUCE

125g softened **butter** (measure using packet)

1 mug (210g) **demerara** or **soft brown sugar**

3 **eggs**

1 tablespoon **golden syrup**

250g **ready-to-eat dried dates**, chopped

1¹⁄₃ mugs (280g) **self-raising flour**

2 tablespoons **water**

50g **butter** (measure using packet)

300ml **double cream**

1 tablespoon **golden syrup**

¹⁄₂ mug (105g) **demerara** or **soft brown sugar**

1 teaspoon **vanilla** extract

1 Preheat the oven to 160°C fan/180°C/gas 4. Grease a 30x20cm dish (needs to be 5cm high).

2 Beat the butter and sugar. Add the eggs, one at a time, and beat well. Stir in the syrup.

3 Add the dates, flour and water and mix well. Pour into the dish and spread out. Place in the oven for 35–40 minutes.

4 To make the toffee sauce, put the butter, cream, syrup, sugar and butter into a saucepan and gently bring to the boil. Simmer until the sugar has dissolved. Add the vanilla extract. Serve with the hot pudding.

   V GF

ALMOND PEAR PAVLOVA WITH CHOCOLATE SAUCE

This is best eaten the day that you make it. It goes very 'gooey' by the next day, but it is still very tasty.

ONE MORE THING: Don't be shy with the chocolate sauce with this one, there is nothing like excess! I've heard that calories don't count when you're eating desserts.

4 **egg** whites

1 mug (225g) **caster sugar**

100g **ground almonds**

½ mug (150ml) **double cream**

100g **milk chocolate**

300ml **double cream**

400g tin **pears**, drained

1 Preheat the oven to 150°C fan/170°C/gas 3. Put some greaseproof paper on a large baking tray.

2 Whisk the egg whites in a clean bowl until they form stiff peaks.

3 Gradually add the sugar and beat until the mixture is smooth and silky. It should be quite stiff.

4 Gently fold in the ground almonds.

5 Tip out onto the tray and spread the meringue into a 30cm round.

6 Put in the oven for 1 hour. After one hour, turn off the heat, but leave the meringue in for another 15 minutes. Take out of the oven; if you leave it in, it will continue to dry out.

7 Meanwhile, make the chocolate sauce. Put the cream in a small saucepan and bring to the boil. Take off the heat and add the broken-up chocolate. Stir until the chocolate melts. Leave to cool.

8 Once the meringue has cooled, whip the cream until stiff and put over the top. Place the drained pears on top of the cream. Drizzle the chocolate sauce over the top just before serving.

WATCH A VIDEO OF MAKING PAVLOVAS AT
NOSHBOOKS.COM/PAVLOVA

index

SAY HELLO TO ALL OUR FAMILIES...

DAVID & HANNAH

We have 3 little girls, Eve 5, Faith 4 and Beth 2. As well as looking after the girls, Hannah works part-time as a GP receptionist and David is a teacher at the local school. Fresh and healthy food is important to us, as is being adventurous. We love recipes that are quick to make and in keeping with our food budget.

BEN & NICOLE

We have 3 kids, Isabella (4), Toby (2) and Poppy (1). Nicole, a full time mum, while Ben runs his own business. We love good food with minimal fuss. If I even mutter the words 'Chicken Pie' Isabella get's crazy excited. I think she might love it more than the colour pink... well...maybe not...but it is a close second!

LEE & SARAH

We are a family with 4 'full of beans' young kids (Jack 2, Lily-May 3, Callum 6, & Emma 8), a husband who seems to be a bigger kid than them all and Sarah a full time mum. We live in Bedford, since relocating from London around 10 years ago. We all enjoy spending time together with friends & visiting new places.

PETER & BERNICE

Not sure what you call off-spring who are 18+, sometimes at home and sometimes not, but we have 3 of these (Josh, Bethany and Ben), plus 1–2 lodgers, so the numbers eating can vary widely. To further complicate catering, the above mix includes veggies, omnivores, carnivores, and some 'fussy-vores'. Dishes which are quick to prepare, exciting to the taste buds, AND economical, are particularly welcome.

DAN & LEENA

We have 3 young boys, Elijah 5, Aaron 4 and Aidan 2. Leena is a full-time stay-at-home mum and Dan works as a social worker. We all love our food and enjoy cooking and eating foods from different countries. At this stage of our lives, days can be very hectic and it would be useful to have recipes that are convenient to prepare and cook, but are also tasty and appealing for all of us.

STEVE & CANDY

Jessica and Joel love spending time with each other, especially around a table of tasty food. Jessica enjoys helping to bake, especially cracking eggs open! Joel enjoys rough and tumbling with his Dad. One of our favourite 'Joy' recipes is 'Spicy Moroccan Lamb Pie'; quick and super tasty.

GARY & NIKKI

We have 3 young children, Emily 4, Naomi 7 and Ethan 9. Life is very busy as a family. Gary works long shifts in London and Nikki is a play leader at a local Pre-School, so not a lot of time to cook. We all love to sit down as a family, but this can be difficult with Gary doing shifts. So looking for easy and quick meals that can be cooked and enjoyed as a family.

JO

I am a busy single mum who works full-time. I have two children, Emily 15 and Oliver 12. We all love to cook and enjoy food with lots of flavour, but that doesn't take too long to get to the plate.

JOE & SARAH

We have 2 young boys, Seth (6) and Jared (4). Both are always

hungry! Cooking for our family needs to be fun, not too time consuming, but yet provide a healthy, hearty meal for us all to enjoy.

ANDY & HEATHER

We have 5 children, Joanna 21, Daniel 19, Bethany 16, Rachel 16 and Nathan 14. 4 of them still live at home and have very healthy appetites. We all like trying different food and, with busy lives, we've found the recipes in this book great, for variety, speed and economy.

ALAN & JO

We are the Layton family: Alan, Jo and grown up children Sam, Rosie and Charlie. We are all very busy, Alan and Jo both working full-time. We love cooking and sharing meals as a family and with our friends. Meals in our house have to be very flexible and elastic, as we are never quite sure who will be in and how many extra people there might be. We loved trying out the recipes, especially gaining lots of new ideas.

LUKE & RACHEL

We have 2 young girls, Samantha is 2 and a half (and loves playing outdoors) and Melody is 1 (and loves playing with her musical giraffe!). They're lots of fun and keep Rach busy at home, whilst Luke goes out to work with young people. Our family love food and love eating together! We both enjoy cooking, but it can be hard to find time in the day to prepare delicious, healthy food and also to find and try out new recipes. So we're looking forward to some new ideas and inspiration!

ADAM & CONNIE

In our family, we have Adam, who's a teacher, myself as full-time Mum and two little girls, Molly 3 and Esme 21 months. Food is a definite pleasure in our household, but fresh ideas do not always come easily. Meals are prepared often in a rush and can be fairly repetitive. Food that is full of flavour and easy to make are the sort of recipes we love.

CONVERSIONS

All of these are approximate conversions, which have either been rounded up or down.

TEMPERATURE

Gas	Fan°C	Oven°C	Oven°F
1	120	140	275
2	130	150	300
3	150	170	325
4	160	180	350
5	170	190	375
6	180	200	400
7	200	220	425
8	210	230	450
9	220	240	475

WEIGHT

Metric	Imperial
15g	1/2 oz
20g	3/4 oz
25g	1 oz
40g	1 1/2 oz
50g	2 oz
70g	2 1/2 oz
75g	3 oz
100g	4 oz
150g	5 oz
175g	6 oz
200g	7 oz
225g	8 oz
250g	9 oz
275g	10 oz
350g	12 oz
450g	1 lb
675g	1 1/2 lb
900g	2 lb

VOLUME

Metric	Imperial
25ml	1 fl oz
50ml	2 fl oz
85ml	3 fl oz
150ml	5 fl oz (1/4 pint)
300ml	10 fl oz (1/2 pint)
450ml	15 fl oz (3/4 pint)
600ml	1 pint
1 litre	1 3/4 pints
1.2 litres	2 pints
1.5 litres	2 1/2 pints
2 litres	3 1/2 pints
2.25 litres	4 pints
2.75 litres	5 pints
4.5 litres	8 pints (1 Gallon)

LENGTH

Metric	Imperial
0.5 cm	1/4 inch
1 cm	1/2 inch
2.5 cm	1 inch
5 cm	2 inches
7.5 cm	3 inches
10 cm	4 inches
15 cm	6 inches
18 cm	7 inches
20 cm	8 inches
23 cm	9 inches
25 cm	10 inches
30 cm	12 inches

COOKING TIMES

BOILING VEGETABLES

Swedes and turnips	2–3cm chunks	20–25 mins
Potatoes	2–3cm chunks	10–15 mins
Parsnips, carrots	cut into 2cm rings	10–15 mins
Cauliflower	broken into little trees	10 mins
Broccoli	broken into little trees	5 mins
Green beans	cut off the stalk and tail	5 mins
Spinach	take off any thick stalks	30 secs–1 min
Leeks	cut into 2cm rings	5 mins
Cabbage	cut into long thin strips	5 mins
Sugar snaps	leave as they are	2 mins
Mangetout	leave as they are	1 min

ROASTING VEGETABLES

Potatoes	cut into 5–6cm chunks	40–50 mins
Butternut squash	peel, cut into 5–6cm chunks	30–40 mins
Parsnips	cut into 4, lengthways	40–45 mins
Sweet potatoes	peel, cut into 5–6cm chunks	40–50 mins
Onions	cut into 6 wedges	40–50 mins
Fennel	cut into 4 wedges	30–40 mins
Tomatoes	cut the skin	20–25 mins
Peppers	remove seeds & stalk and slice	25 mins

THE NOSH FAMILY

NOSH Books began when Ben went to uni. He couldn't, and wouldn't, cook! Only when the realities of uni dawned, and he realised how hungry he was, did he begin to show an interest. So Joy wrote 'NOSH for Students'. Fast forward 18 years and Ben can (thankfully) cook and he now works, along with the rest of the family, on creating the NOSH series of books.

It is a real family effort, Joy is the author, Ben the photographer and designer, Tim the food stylist, recipe tester and sales manager and Ron holds the whole thing together and keeps everyone on track (most of the time)!

THANKS

A special thanks to all our volunteer families for testing all of our recipes for us, we really appreciate it.

Thanks to my very good friend Fran Maciver for proofreading the book.

Bella's tea party - thanks to Bella, Grace, Ella, Hannah, Evie, Faith, Beth and Toby.

Teens' video night - thanks to Sam, Bethany, Jemima, Rachel and Nathan.

Getting kids involved - thanks to Ollie and Emily.

Printed in China
Published by: inTRADE (GB) ltd.
ISBN: 9780956746412
1st edition: September 2017
2nd edition: February 2021
Contact: us@noshbooks.com

Author: Joy May
Food Styling: Tim May
Photography and Design: Ben May
Editor: Ron May
Proofreading: Fran Maciver

supported by

Built better to last longer

WÜSTHOF

KENWOOD